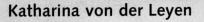

Katharina von der Leyen

BARRON'S *Illustrated Guide to*

140 DOG BREEDS

> "Every man is a Napoleon to his dog. That is
> why dogs are so popular."
>
> Aldous Huxley

Note of Thanks

I have gotten to know a great many dogs during my lifetime, and there are few other things I have approached with the same concentration and intensity of interest. Still, I would not have been able to write this book without the patient help of veterinarians, dog breeders, breed examiners, and show judges in many countries. I cannot possibly list all the dog owners and trainers who again and again had to put up with being asked the most outlandish questions. But I must express special thanks to my veterinarian, Jan Groth, who gave unstintingly of his time and lent me all the books needed; to Frau Balzereit, Frau Reuter, and Herr Kleinwächter of the Dog Boarding Home Antonienwald Werner in Wagenfeld, who took at least as good care of me as of my dogs and who considered no dog problem too thorny, no question too stupid, and no deadline too soon; to Frau Waltraut Elsner, who introduced me to Pugs; to Frau Schmidt of the Weimaraner Club; to Margit J. Mayer; to Herr Josef Schaller of the Belgian Shepherd Club; to Mr. Karl Miller of Los Angeles; to Anne Urbauer, who doesn't even like dogs particularly, and still lent me stylistic and moral support; and to my grandmother, who passed her addiction to dogs on to me at an early age, and thus is responsible for all this.

A Cautionary Tale

For a whole year, I watched a woman come to the park every morning, equipped with bicycle, tennis racket, and yellow ball, to provide her Border Collie with the physical exercise he needed. She would come bicycling as fast as she could, and once she reached the open field, she would start hitting the ball so far that tennis professionals could only have applauded. The dog never took his eyes off her for a second, and as soon as the ball went flying, off he went after it to close in on it, and grab it. Nothing could distract him, not even another dog. He was intent on returning the ball to his mistress as quickly as possible so that the game could start all over again.

After an hour or so, the woman's right wrist would refuse further service, and she would get back on her bike to pedal home behind her fleet-footed dog, as fast as her quadriceps permitted.

When I asked her one day why she had chosen this particular kind of dog, she said she had decided on it after seeing the movie *Babe*. Nobody had warned her how much work and exercise this breed needed. This was her first Border Collie and, she was determined, the last.

Border Collies are working dogs obsessed with performance and filled with incredible energy. They can't help being this way. On the contrary, for centuries these qualities were systematically bred into these herding dogs. Neither can they help the fame the movie brought them, nor the consequences of their popularity. Deprived of the use they were intended for, Border Collies, now turned family pets, have to learn to make do with herding children, other animals, or tennis balls.

A Dog Made to Order

Whether the next 12 years or so will be a time of delight for you and your dog depends entirely on your choosing a breed that fits your way of life. Almost all the problems between dogs and their owners result from the simple fact that the two are ill-matched. Most people pick a dog for its looks and pay no attention to the qualities it was originally bred for. Then, for the rest of the animal's life, the owner keeps trying desperately to change the dog's inborn character traits. "The dog keeps digging up my garden," an avid gardener complains. Of course it does; after all it is a Dachshund, a breed developed to dig rodents out of their subterranean tunnels. Digging is in its genes.

"He's so mean with other dogs," a lady wails, who would like the company of other ladies out with their dogs when she goes for walks with hers. Of course her dog is aggressive; it is a Fox Terrier, bred to kill foxes and martens instantly in their lairs. Ferociousness is in its genes.

"He's so arrogant toward my friends," sighs a man who likes to entertain. Of course the dog is arrogant; after all it's a Borzoi, which was not bred to be a companion dog, but a fierce and independent hunter of wolves. Hautiness is in its genes.

Most dog breeds were created for one simple reason, to make it easier for two species as dissimilar as man and dog to live together. In the case of working breeds, those instincts and qualities were encouraged to assist the dogs in their necessary tasks. In companion dogs, what counted were friendliness, love of children, and beauty. (Dogs, of course, don't care in the least how we look, which is one of their great qualities.) There is a breed to fit just about every kind of person. The gardener would probably be much happier with a dignified Pekinese, and the man who likes to entertain, would be better off with an affectionate Labrador Retriever. But they didn't know any better.

You are in a better position to establish a happy relationship with a dog because you can select precisely the breed that is right for your way of life. It is possible, of course, to modify almost any temperament and breed-specific quality through patient, firm, and consistent training. But life with a dog will be much easier and less frustrating if you start with a breed that is at least somewhat adapted to your desires and circumstances.

The athletic, highly intelligent Australian Shepherd was developed to fit the specific needs of hard-working cowherds.

Of course, there are exceptions to any rule. Just because someone swears his Afghan is the friendliest and most playful dog in the world, you should not go out and buy one for yourself, hoping to chance on a similarly atypical individual. I also know two Border Collies who are so gentle and restrained they must have swallowed an overdose of Valium at birth, and a Weimaraner with about as much hunting instinct as a blanket. These dogs, which would be totally useless as working dogs, make wonderful family pets. But they are rare exceptions. Anyone who insists on selecting a dog purely on the basis of what appeals to his or her sense of beauty can't be helped. But remember that hundreds of thousands of pets bought for their looks end up in animal shelters every year, and are eventually put down because they are not suitable for adoption.

So You Think You Want a Dog?

The problem is that a dog is not some kind of commodity that you can buy and then forget about for a while. Dogs are expensive. They smell, shed, take up time, and make work. The purchase price, which can range from several hundred to more than a thousand dollars, is only part of the expense. Don't forget the ongoing costs of food, veterinary services, liability insurance, muzzles (at least one is usually chewed up), as well as periodic visits to the canine beauty salon for breeds that have to be shorn or trimmed. Dogs take up time, demand patience, and can be a strain on your nerves. Puppies urinate everywhere, chew on furniture, knock over the garbage pail, and spread the oil left in empty tuna fish cans over your new sofa. They have no manners. They are flatulent, like to roll in the most dis-

The Dachshund is not a couch potato, but a hardy, working breed used for hunting.

gusting stuff, bite other dogs and joggers, and they get diarrhea on the most expensive carpets in the house. It's a nuisance to have to take a puppy out every two hours in the pouring rain, hoping it will relieve itself. It's even worse when the puppy pays attention only to the interesting smells along the way and then, finally, empties its bladder in the warm house, creating a veritable lake in the hallway. It's not easy to resist the urge to strangle the little beast after it has turned your favorite shoes into sandals, and it's even less easy to remain

stern and consistent when the culprit sits in front of you wagging its tail and looks up at you, head atilt, with an expression of surprise, and not a trace of guilt. It tries your patience to clean the house for guests and then watch the dog race through the rooms with muddy paws, throw up on the carpet, wave its tail over the coffee table, and shake itself next to the sofa, sending loose hair flying. It's difficult to try to find a veterinarian in the middle of the night.

It's hard to never forget, when training a dog, that we are dealing with a creature that sees the world through eyes that are fundamentally different from ours. It's difficult to imagine what it's like to be in the dog's place. We expect miraculous things from man's best friend, things we see in the movies, and we punish our dogs if they don't live up to our expectations. Sometimes we even find it hard to scratch the dog's ears after it has been waiting all day for us to come home.

To make a long story short, owning a dog involves both pleasure *and* responsibility. It means taking full responsibility for the life of another creature. Unlike a child, a dog never becomes independent. To a dog, for as long as it lives, its master is the entire universe, the source of everything from food and water to love, medical care, and bad weather. Unlike a child, a dog does not grow up to become gradually less dependent until, someday, it can be let go. Letting go, in the case of a dog, can be very sudden, and it is always final.

How to Find the Right Dog

If you are still determined to live with a dog, the next step is to look for the dog that is right for you. And that is, after all, not so very difficult. This book is meant to make the choice as easy as possible by listing dog breeds alphabetically and offering concise answers to the questions you should be asking. The heading "Common Health Problems" warns about a breed's susceptibility to certain diseases. Of course, not every dog of the breed will actually develop them, and, conversely, dogs do get diseases not mentioned under their breed. The prices given are approximate only, to give you some idea of what to expect. Prices also vary if you purchase a dog in another country.

Make a list of the qualities that matter most to you in a dog. Try to overcome preconceived notions about sizes and breeds. Perhaps you never even considered looking at breed XY. Why? Is it because a friend once said this was the most idiotic kind of dog in the world and he had to know what he was talking about because his aunt once had such a dog? If you generalize too readily from a single experience, or accept one person's opinion, you are necessarily ignoring hundreds of other breeds and experiences, and you will be depriving yourself of too many options. You think that only a big dog is a real dog? In dogs, as in people, physical size is no indication of other qualities, and the smallest often have the greatest personalities. Try to be as honest as possible, even if that means that the list of compatible breeds keeps shrinking as you find answers to your questions in this book. Since you are one person—or one family—and 140 breeds are described in the following pages, the process of elimination is inevitable. So what are the points you should consider?

Are you a neophyte in canine matters, or do you have some experience with dogs? Luckily, most dogs, but not all of them, do fine with first-time owners. In the case of some breeds, having experience in handling dogs is essential.

How important is it that your dog get along well with children? If there are a lot of kids in your neighborhood, this is an important question, not to mention if you have children of your own. If you have practically no contact with children, there is of course no problem.

Are you looking for a small, medium-sized, or large dog? Small dogs don't need much exercise, and obedience training is not so crucial (though it never does any harm). Neighbors are usually not afraid of small dogs, and it is easier to clean up after small dogs and take them on trips. Medium-sized dogs need at least one good walk a day, and they have to be trained. They generally don't intimidate neighbors and can be

taken along almost anywhere. Large dogs need a yard and extensive walks. They have to be very obedient, and even then neighbors are often afraid of them, or landlords may object to them. It is also more difficult to travel with a big dog. The cost of keeping a dog increases with the animal's size, and so does the labor of cleaning up after it. Reliable obedience training is also crucial for the largest dogs, which also need a yard and

These puppies, with their loose folds of skin, will grow up into muscular Boxers.

lengthy walks. Neighbors and landlords are usually scared of them, as is anyone who might want to break into your house. Traveling with very big dogs is difficult. They create quite a lot of dirt and are expensive to keep. (The size given in the descriptions, by the way, indicates height at the withers.)

How often are you willing to vacuum? What kind of coat would you like your dog to have? Having a dog with long hair means a lot of work. Short-haired breeds normally require practically no extra work. (However, there are dogs that shed heaps of hair constantly, even though their fur isn't very long.)

How much time do you have for walks and how athletic are you? Almost all dogs love long walks and a lot of other exercise, but there are some breeds that are perfectly content if they are taken out for half an hour. Dogs with extremely short noses or very thick coats can have trouble breathing, or suffer a heart attack, if they are worked too hard in very hot weather.

How much time and effort are you willing to devote to obedience training? Some breeds behave fairly well without much training at all, but for others obedience lessons have to be reinforced as long as the dog lives. Some dogs take more advantage than others of their master's inexperience in dealing with dogs.

Do you want your dog to be friendly toward strangers, act as a watchdog and bark, or act with arrogant aloofness? In most situations, it is a good idea for a dog to at least alert you when strangers approach. If, however, you keep an "open house" with a constant stream of visitors and children coming and going all the time, you'd go crazy with a dog that thought its major purpose in life was to guard the house.

Once you have considered these questions—as well as others you may have—the descriptions in this book will help you find the dog that fits your requirements. Aspects of dog ownership that are particularly important for new pet owners, such as Grooming, Required Exercise, and Suitability for City Living, are also represented in graph form using a point system. The points run from 1 to 10, where 1 (or no) point means that the breed in question needs practically no grooming or exercise or is not suitable for a city apartment. The number of points assigned is also reflected in the size of the colored area in a given graph.

Where to Find the Right Dog

There are several ways of acquiring a purebred dog: from a conscientious breeder, from an irresponsible breeder, through an advertisement in a newspaper or magazine, from an animal shelter, or from someone you know. In Germany alone, about 550,000 puppies are produced annually to satisfy the demand of animal lovers. About 60 percent of these puppies are purebreds, but only about 120,000 of them are from litters registered with the German Association of Dog Breeders. Breeding dogs is big business, and there are

A dog is a gift to be treasured for as long as it lives, not just while it is a puppy.

INTRODUCTION

And now, off to a light-colored sofa!

plenty of "wild" breeders prepared to meet the huge demand for dogs, people who belong to no dog clubs, or to fictitious ones, and who pay little or no attention to breed standards. In addition, there are puppy mills in countries like Czechoslovakia, Poland, and Hungary that mass breed dogs as cheaply as possible, keep them in tiny boxes, and then ship the puppies to Germany by the truckload.

In contrast, responsible breeders are dedicated to maintaining and improving the breeds they deal with. They don't breed a bitch more than once a year; they allow their dog club to examine bitches and puppies, and they make sure their grown dogs are healthy, cheerful, and checked medically to ensure that no hereditary diseases are developing. A good breeder sees to it that a pregnant bitch and her newborn pup-

pies receive good care, and goes to great lengths to find good homes for the young dogs he or she has raised so carefully. A potential new owner will be asked all kinds of questions about his or her way of life and ability to satisfy the needs of the young dog. A good breeder never tries to talk you into getting a puppy, even if it's the last of the litter and he or she is about to leave on vacation. Only unscrupulous breeders do that kind of thing, and unfortunately they don't wear any tag identifying them as such. So, you have to act as your own Sherlock Holmes.

Unscrupulous breeders often refuse to let you see their adult dogs, making some excuse like "the mother of the puppies is out being walked." They may be raising four, five, or even twenty different breeds, all of which may be kept in separate, clean kennels, but these dogs have little contact with humans except at feeding time. An irresponsible breeder doesn't worry about which of the puppies might be temperamentally most suitable for the future owner, because he or she doesn't know the individual puppies well enough. Besides, all that matters is that the buyer makes a decision quickly, and takes one of the dogs. Profit-oriented breeders also quickly take up fashionable breeds, as soon as a dog can fetch $1,000 or more. Puppies from such breeders may be cheaper to buy than ones from responsible breeders, who invest a lot of time and money in raising dogs. But the bargain tends to turn sour in the long run. Poor-quality dogs can cost a fortune in veterinarian's bills, and puppies that were taken from their mother too early and didn't have any close contact with humans early on may develop into dogs that bite out of fear. Such dogs usually end up in the animal shelter since, after all, you can't take a chance with the safety of your kids.

Reaching the Right Decision

So take plenty of time, time to decide which breed really matches your requirements, time to find a breeder whom you feel you can trust and whose dogs you like, and time to select a dog that is cheerful and well adjusted.

You probably took your time getting to know your life's companion before you gave your final "yes," so why should you hurry now? A dog's life lasts 10, 12, 15 years, longer than many marriages these days. Why, then, should you rush into a decision? The lives of humans and dogs have been intertwined for more than 20,000 years, and that will still be the case six months from now.

The connection between man and dog is the oldest, longest lasting, and perhaps most complex relationship between two different species in all of history. If there were no dogs, we'd have to invent them. They are cheerful, courageous, and faithful. They embody, in Lord Byron's words, "all the virtues of man, without his vices." Medical studies have shown that the presence of a dog can relieve stress and lower blood pressure and that heart patients live longer if there is a dog in the house. One hardly needs mention the ruddier complexion of dog owners who spend more time in the fresh air than most other people. Dogs have always been the unquestioning accomplices in all of man's enterprises from war to games of Frisbee. Their sense of humor is disarming, their sensitivity overwhelming, and their enthusiasm infallible. (None of my dogs ever displayed anything less than utter delight at the meals I offered them, whether the menu included a handful of popcorn or some chunks of raw carrot. Surely no husband is as easy to please.) They earn their keep as rescuers of people in distress and as detectives, as well as by acting as mouthpieces for the deaf and mute, and as eyes for the blind. They keep the lonely company and listen to us without ever contradicting us. We can say the most idiotic things, and our dog will wag its tail politely and act as though it was interested in what we have to say. He makes us try to find a tree in the middle of a big city, and allows us to view rabbit holes and joggers with completely different eyes.

Perhaps that is the greatest contribution dogs make to our lives: they make the world we live in more humane.

An important note about pronouns: Throughout the book, we have used the word "it" to refer to specific dogs or breeds of dog. This was a simple editorial decision so as to avoid the awkward "he or she" throughout, and is in no way intended to take away from the importance of dogs in all our lives.

AFFENPINSCHER

Height	10 in (25 cm)
Weight	9 lbs (4 kg)
Coat	hard, dense, abundant
Color	bluish gray, black and tan, grayish black, red

Grooming

1	2	3	4	5	6	7	8	9	10

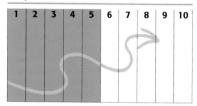

Required Exercise

1	2	3	4	5	6	7	8	9	10

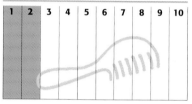

Suitability for City Living

1	2	3	4	5	6	7	8	9	10

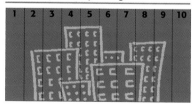

Common Health Problems

Suitable for first-time owners

The origin of the **AFFENPINSCHER** is shrouded in darkness. The breed seems to have existed in Germany, or at least in Europe, as early as the sixteenth century. The Affenpinscher was first used to catch rats, but ended up being a lap dog. It is a wonderful small dog for someone living in an apartment, but it is a barker and a showoff. If given the slightest chance, it will exploit its master's every weakness and take over the entire household. The Affenpinscher takes itself very seriously, and expects everyone else to do the same. It is a loving and devoted pet, but also very tough. It has no tolerance for teasing and will, without pity, attack anyone or anything that irritates it. If things don't go according to its wishes, it can get very sulky. There may be quite a few trying moments before an equilibrium is established between master and dog, but taking the trouble is well worthwhile. The Affenpinscher should not be spoiled because, when it is, it is likely to become an impossible tyrant. But this highly intelligent dog responds very positively to firm and consistent training. What the Affenpinscher lacks in size, it makes up in personality, and this personality deserves to be respected.

AFGHAN HOUND

Height	25–27 in (63–68 cm)
Weight	48–59 lbs (22–27 kg)
Coat	long and silky
Color	all colors permitted: unicolor, black and tan, and domino (dark saddle and face with lighter feathering on legs and head)

If you picture yourself with a dog that responds eagerly to your commands, the **AFGHAN HOUND** is not for you. The Afghan is an aristocrat with a regal air and an arrogant bearing. It was bred more than 6,000 years ago to run down gazelles, hares, and leopards in the deserts of Afghanistan, while the hunters followed on horseback. This history explains why this dog requires so much physical exercise. The Afghan has excellent sight and is completely independent. And here lies the potential problem. Training a dog of this kind takes practically superhuman skills, and professional help may be advisable because this breed needs to be handled with great sensitivity and patience. If an Afghan feels unjustly treated, it stops cooperating and practically cuts off contact with the world around it. Yet it thrives on affection, is a clown at heart, and constantly tries to please its master. It should not be blamed if its hunting instinct takes over and leads it astray now and then. The gorgeous coat requires constant care if it is not to degenerate into a matted mess. Anyone considering buying an Afghan should be fully aware that this dog, though the picture of elegance and beauty, is not a decorative accessory, but a tough and determined hunter even now.

Grooming

1	2	3	4	5	6	7	8	9	10

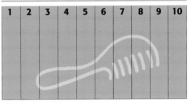

Required Exercise

1	2	3	4	5	6	7	8	9	10

Suitability for City Living

1	2	3	4	5	6	7	8	9	10

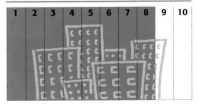

Common Health Problems

hip dysplasia, cataracts

For experienced dog owners

AIREDALE TERRIER

Height	23–24 in (58–61 cm)
Weight	approximately 44 lbs (20 kg)
Coat	wiry, hard, dense
Color	black-grizzle, with bright tan markings

Grooming

1	2	3	4	5	6	7	8	9	10

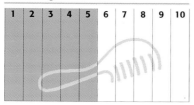

Required Exercise

1	2	3	4	5	6	7	8	9	10

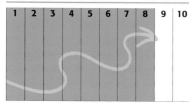

Suitability for City Living

1	2	3	4	5	6	7	8	9	10

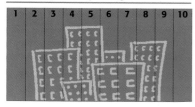

Common Health Problems

occasional hip dysplasia

For experienced dog owners

Like most terriers, the **AIREDALE TERRIER** is an English breed, and it embodies the typical virtues of an English gentleman. It is always dignified, patient, intelligent, reliable, and loyal. The most sensible of all terriers, it was not bred to burrow after small animals, but to hunt bear and wolves. The Airedale is an active dog, but it adapts quite well to the city as long as it gets enough exercise. It has a well-developed guarding instinct without being a yapper. In fact, it is really an all-purpose dog that will do just about anything. It has been used not only as a hunting dog, but also as a seeing-eye dog, a police dog, a narcotics detective, and a watchdog. Today, however, its main role is as companion dog, which surely does not do justice to its abilities. It loves to play and horse around with children and needs a lot of attention from its master. Owners of Airedales sound not unlike religious fanatics whenever the conversation turns to their favorite breed—to them the only true and worthwhile dog. The popularity of the Airedale goes back quite some time and peaked in the 1970s; luckily the breed has been able to recover from that boom. If given half a chance, this terrier will prove itself a true and loyal friend no matter what the circumstances. It is not size alone that has earned it the epithet "king of terriers."

Height	25–28 in (64–71 cm)
Weight	66–88 lbs (30–40 kg)
Coat	thick, double-coated, with guard hair
Color	red, brindle; color set off against white background; often with a black mask.

Grooming

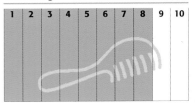

| 1 | 2 | 3 | 4 | 5 | 6 | 7 | 8 | 9 | 10 |

Required Exercise

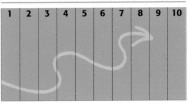

| 1 | 2 | 3 | 4 | 5 | 6 | 7 | 8 | 9 | 10 |

Suitability for City Living

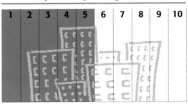

| 1 | 2 | 3 | 4 | 5 | 6 | 7 | 8 | 9 | 10 |

The **AKITA** is the national dog of Japan and resembles Nordic breeds in type. It goes back about three hundred years and was originally developed for use as a fighting, hunting, and guard dog. Nowadays, it is valued almost exclusively as a companion and family dog, especially in England and the United States. But this inactive way of life often seems to leave the dog dissatisfied and frustrated. Though peaceful, docile, and dignified by nature, some Akitas are very aggressive toward other dogs. As a former working dog, the Akita needs a great deal of outdoor activity, as well as thorough and fair obedience training if it is going to be part of a family. Because of its past as a hunter and its fearlessness, it has to respond to commands with absolute reliability. Fans of the breed always point to the Akita's superior intelligence and its eagerness to please its master. The Akita has a memory like an elephant's for any instance of unfair or unjust treatment, and is therefore not a pet that can be ignored when convenient. It may prove problematic with children. In the case of Akitas, it is essential to buy from a reputable breeder, because if the dog was raised without adequate care, or was poorly socialized as a puppy, you may end up with a domineering and aggressive Akita.

Common Health Problems

hip dysplasia, dislocation of kneecap, thyroid problems, eye disease, tendency to develop eczema

For experienced dog owners

ALASKAN MALAMUTE

Height	male: 25 in (64 cm); female: 23 in (59 cm)
Weight	male: approximately 85 lbs (38.5 kg); female: 75 lbs (34 kg)
Coat	medium long, coarse guard hair with a dense, soft undercoat
Color	all colors are permitted; normally light gray to black, with white belly and white markings on face, legs, and feet

Grooming

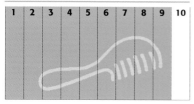

Required Exercise

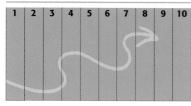

Suitability for City Living

The **ALASKAN MALAMUTE** was bred centuries ago by a nomadic Eskimo tribe called Mahlemuts, who needed a very strong, but not necessarily very fast, dog for pulling sleds. It is the workhorse among dogs. Because of its unquestioning loyalty and devotion it makes a perfect home and family dog—better than any of the other Arctic sled dog breeds. This is an intelligent and reliable dog, sturdy and untiring. It is normally friendly toward strangers, but should be watched around cats and other small animals. The Malamute is affected by the heat. It needs a lot of physical activity and should be kept where it has the run of a yard, or in the country. After all, it was bred to be a working dog. Malamutes are independent and very strong, and they can become overbearing if they are not trained from an early age with firmness and consistency. They hardly smell at all, but they have another drawback: They lose their thick undercoat in the course of spring and summer. If the dog is not professionally trimmed, the amount of hair it sheds is enough to drive any housewife over the edge. Malamutes are ideal for active outdoors people who want a large, strong dog. If well brought up, the Malamute is an impressive and almost perfect companion.

Common Health Problems

hip dysplasia, zinc deficiency, thyroid problems, achondroplasia

For experienced dog owners

Height	male: approximately 16 in (40 cm); female: approximately 15 in (37 cm)
Weight	24–29 lbs (11–13 kg)
Coat	long, silky, wavy, and abundant
Color	solid black, black with points, cream, roan, black and white, orange and white, tan, tricolor (black, tan, and white), and others

Grooming

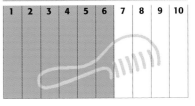

Required Exercise

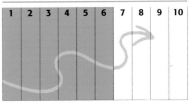

Suitability for City Living

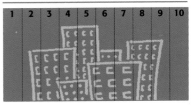

Common Health Problems

hip dysplasia, dislocation of the kneecap, epilepsy, tonsilitis, retinal atrophy, allergies, heart disease

Suitable for first-time owners

Like all spaniels, the **AMERICAN COCKER SPANIEL** is descended from Spanish hunting dogs, which are also the forebears of setters and the larger modern spaniels. The American Cocker Spaniel is the smallest of the sporting breeds. Over the years, though, the dog's looks have acquired much more importance than its hunting talents. American Cocker Spaniels were bred more and more for the show bench, with little or no attention paid to their intelligence. Breeders vied with each other trying to produce glamorously feathered champions. The breed became hugely popular, but its days of working in fields and forests were over. This is what typically happens when a breed catches on and becomes fashionable. Luckily, the American Cocker Spaniel's outstanding qualities of character have survived in some lines despite the emphasis on beautiful appearance. The Cocker is an even-tempered, friendly, and loving dog of great charm. It gets along well with children and always tries to please its master. Its most striking physical characteristic is its thick, luxurious coat, which has to be taken care of conscientiously. One important thing to keep in mind is that the American Cocker Spaniel makes highly efficient use of the food it eats. That is why you have to watch how much it eats and not give in to it, no matter how irresistibly its beautiful eyes look up at you at the dinner table.

AMERICAN STAFFORDSHIRE TERRIER

Height	16–18 in (40–46 cm)
Weight	37–44 lbs (17–20 kg)
Coat	hard, smooth, and glossy
Color	all colors permitted, but more than 80 percent white is undesirable

Grooming

1	2	3	4	5	6	7	8	9	10

Required Exercise

1	2	3	4	5	6	7	8	9	10

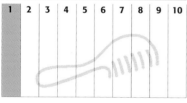

Suitability for City Living

1	2	3	4	5	6	7	8	9	10

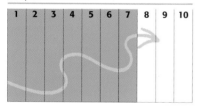

Common Health Problems

hip dysplasia

For experienced dog owners

The **AMERICAN STAFFORDSHIRE TERRIER** belongs to the fighting breeds, and to the tender-hearted animal lover, its history is a nightmare. These dogs were bred for use in the bloody sport of dog fighting, and in popular imagination they are therefore associated with virulent cruelty. But this reputation does not do the breed justice. The American Staffordshire is generally calm and friendly and has a dignified, self-confident air. It is affectionate, easy to train, playful, and at the same time absolutely fearless. It is normally friendly toward strangers, as long as its people are around. But it is not to be trusted around cats and other dogs. If it gets into a fight, this dog, like any other terrier, is out to kill. You should, therefore, never allow unsupervised dog encounters. The short hair requires little care, and if the Staffordshire gets regular, long walks, it can easily be kept in the city. Though strong-willed, it is easy to lead if it has had consistent, fair, and early obedience training. Anybody who resorts to physical punishment, however, will rue the day. This breed should never be trained as a guard dog; its natural guarding instinct is strong enough. Anyone who owns an American Staffordshire owes it to the breed to spend all the necessary time and effort teaching the dog because every nonaggressive, well-behaved dog of this breed will help counteract the hysteria many people experience at the mere mention of fighting dogs.

Height	19–23 in (48–58 cm)
Weight	48–55 lbs (22–25 kg)
Coat	short, dense, glossy
Color	black with yellow to reddish shading and symmetrical white markings

The **APPENZELL MOUNTAIN DOG** is an old Swiss breed. It was kept by farmers because it is an outstanding herding dog of unparalleled watchfulness and because it can also be used for pulling. In earlier times, it hauled milk and cheese from the mountain valleys to the towns in small carts. This dog is a real extrovert and always keeps busy. Laziness is totally foreign to the Appenzell. If there are no cattle to herd, it will guard house, yard, or a baby carriage with great zeal and absolute fearlessness. It is a barker, but not in an annoying way, suspicious of strangers, but devoted to its people. It is happiest outdoors, where it can keep busy and look after "important matters." That is why it is not a candidate for living in an apartment.

Grooming

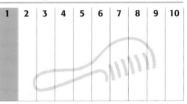

Required Exercise

Suitability for City Living

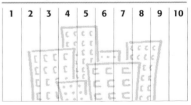

Common Health Problems

Suitable for first-time owners

AUSTRALIAN CATTLE DOG

Height	17–19 in (43–48 cm)
Weight	35–48 lbs (16–22 kg)
Coat	short and hard
Color	blue or red brindle with many white hairs mixed in; patches of pure color ranging from coal black to pure white and any color between

Grooming

1	2	3	4	5	6	7	8	9	10

Required Exercise

1	2	3	4	5	6	7	8	9	10

Suitability for City Living

1	2	3	4	5	6	7	8	9	10

Common Health Problems

For experienced dog owners

The **AUSTRALIAN CATTLE DOG** was created in the mid-nineteenth century by crossing Collies, the Dingo, Bull Terriers, and Dalmatians because the Australians needed a tough cow dog. At that time, Australia was sparsely settled, and the few cattlemen had to find a way to drive their herds from one end of the continent to the other. While the Americans solved a similar problem by producing cowboys, the Australians fashioned this masterpiece of genetic manipulation to achieve a specific goal. The Australian Cattle Dog may not win any beauty prizes, but it fulfills its function perfectly. It is a compact, rugged dog of inexhaustible energy, and it is capable of the most amazing leaps and twists from a standing position, physical attributes needed to keep stubborn cattle moving. Their strength and indifference to discomfort and pain are legendary, and it is therefore important to keep close tabs on them. A sick Cattle Dog will go on working for days without giving any sign of ill health. The Australian Cattle Dog should not be kept as a family dog. Though easily trained, its need for activity, its workaholic temperament, and its conscientious nature can be satisfied only if it can spend its days herding cattle through the countryside. This is a job it is always ready and eager for, and takes extremely seriously. The Australian Cattle Dog is tough, loyal, flexible, and possessive; it is not a dog for first-time owners. It requires more than just food and petting. This dog requires real management.

Height	male: 18–23 in (45–58 cm); female: 17–21 in (43–53 cm)
Weight	29–48 lbs (13–22 kg)
Coat	abundant, of medium length
Color	blue merle, black, red merle, red; with or without white or tan markings

Grooming

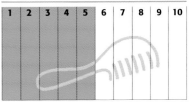

1	2	3	4	5	6	7	8	9	10

Required Exercise

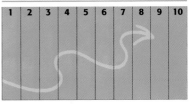

1	2	3	4	5	6	7	8	9	10

Suitability for City Living

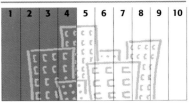

1	2	3	4	5	6	7	8	9	10

Despite its name, the **AUSTRALIAN SHEPHERD** is a thoroughly American dog. It was probably brought to this continent, along with the mustang, by the Spaniards, who dominated the wool trade and imported Australian sheep around the turn of the century. This "dog with spirit eyes," as the Indians called it because of its often multicolored eyes, was regarded as a highly intelligent, reliable herding dog and a loyal family dog, ready to defend those in its charge to the death. This is still an accurate description of the breed. American cowboys still use this herding dog to drive cattle, a fact not to be forgotten by anyone thinking of getting an Australian Shepherd as a family dog. An Aussie that is bored is a disaster because it gets nervous and restless, climbs any fence, opens any door, and chews anything it can find. But whatever your situation, if you can offer it enough exercise, fun, and adventure, you will have a wonderful companion that is easy to teach, full of curiosity, tireless, and sport-loving. These qualities also make it an excellent playmate for children. The Aussie is affectionate and loving with those it knows, but suspicious of strangers, and thus a good watchdog.

Common Health Problems

hip dysplasia, deafness in merle-colored dogs

For experienced dog owners

AUSTRALIAN TERRIER

Height	10 in (25 cm)
Weight	approximately 13 lbs (6 kg)
Coat	hard, straight, weatherproof; with a soft undercoat
Color	blue and tan, solid red (puppies are black at birth)

Grooming

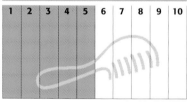

Required Exercise

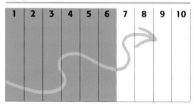

Suitability for City Living

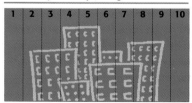

Common Health Problems

Suitable for first-time owners

The **AUSTRALIAN TERRIER** is one of the quietest, most obedient, and most modest terriers, but it does not lack its cousins' toughness, pluck, and intelligence. This is a courageous, robust, and cheerful little dog that probably resulted from crossing Cairn, Yorkshire, and Dandie Dinmont Terriers. It was exhibited at a dog show for the first time in Melbourne in 1880.

The Australian Terrier is an almost perfect apartment dog. It adapts beautifully to any situation, is loyal, charming, and happy, and an alert watchdog without being a yapper. It never gets into fights the way many other terriers do. It approaches strangers with caution, but is friendly toward other animals. Although it is a lively dog, it is never hyperactive and does not need especially long walks, though it loves to be out with its people. It is a quick learner, easy to train, and an equally good choice for country life as for a city apartment. Luckily this breed has thus far escaped becoming fashionable, and you can hardly go wrong choosing an Australian Terrier.

Height	16–17 in (40–42.5 cm)
Weight	20–24 lbs (9–11 kg)
Coat	short, silky
Color	red with white, tricolor, black and white, tiger brindle

The **BASENJI** is one of the oldest dog breeds in existence, and was depicted more than 4,000 years ago in Egyptian tombs as the Pharaohs' favorite dog. It is still found in Zaire and the Sudan, where it is used for hunting. The most remarkable thing about this dog is that it does not bark. Instead it makes noises that are impossible to describe. They resemble something like a chortle or a yodel, happy sounds normally reserved for special occasions or special friends. The Basenji has an excellent nose and is very purposeful. It also has a great sense of humor and a cat-like grace of movement. It is very active and needs extensive walks. It has a pretty high-stepping gait, and when in an exuberant mood it leaps and jumps, looking for all the world like a small, shiny-coated deer. The Basenji is practically odor-free and very clean—a delight to any housewife—and has to be part of the family. If it is left alone too much or does not have enough to do, it can become destructive, or will climb over any fence. (Sometimes it even climbs up trees.) Anyone owning a Basenji has to make sure he or she always keeps one step ahead of this smart dog. Although quite obstinate, the Basenji responds well to consistent training.

Grooming

1	2	3	4	5	6	7	8	9	10

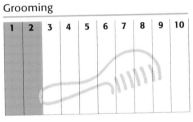

Required Exercise

1	2	3	4	5	6	7	8	9	10

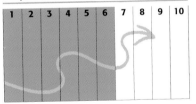

Suitability for City Living

1	2	3	4	5	6	7	8	9	10

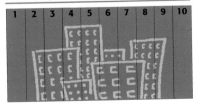

Common Health Problems

hernia, kidney problems

For experienced dog owners

BASSETT HOUND

Height	approximately 15 in (39 cm)
Weight	40–51 lbs (18–23 kg)
Coat	smooth, short, dense
Color	base color is white with brown, black, or sand-colored patches; all recognized hound colors

Grooming

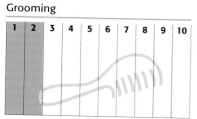

Required Exercise

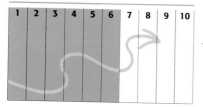

Suitability for City Living

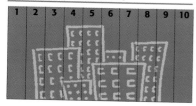

Common Health Problems

spinal problems, ear infections, eyelid abnormalities

Suitable for first-time owners

The **BASSET HOUND** is one of the gentlest of all dogs. Some Bassets are dignified; others are clowns, but all of them are friendly and trustworthy. A Basset adores its master and loves children in particular, going so far as to put up stoically with being dressed like a doll or pushed around in a baby carriage. It cares more for its people than anything else in the world. That is why it should always be included in family activities, and also why it adapts especially well to city or apartment living. But it does have to get a lot of exercise, even though it gives the impression of not enjoying so much exertion. A fat Basset Hound will develop major health problems.

The Basset is a direct descendent of the Bloodhound and has inherited its fabulous nose from this ancestor of all hounds. Thorough and patient obedience training is crucial so that you can be sure that your Basset will come when called, even when following an interesting scent. Bassets can be extremely obstinate, but often display a real sense of humor even while disobeying; they hardly ever present a real problem. The Basset is a dog of substance, physically as well as mentally, and deserves to be treated with respect.

Height	male: 20 in (50 cm); female: 18 in (45 cm)
Weight	approximately 66 lbs (30 kg)
Coat	dense, short, fairly hard
Color	all shades of red; dark red also with black-tipped hair

The **BAVARIAN MOUNTAIN HOUND** was first developed in the mid-nineteenth century from crossing the old Bavarian Hound with the Hanover Hound. This breed is kept exclusively by hunters and is not suited for living as a pure family or companion dog. It is a physically tough dog with outstanding hunting instincts. It usually works on a long lead because once it is on a trail, it is oblivious to whether its master is able to follow it over rough terrain. To add to the hunter's difficulties, the Bavarian Mountain Hound is also an agile climber.

Grooming

1	2	3	4	5	6	7	8	9	10

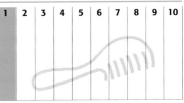

Required Exercise

1	2	3	4	5	6	7	8	9	10

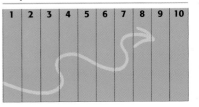

Suitability for City Living

1	2	3	4	5	6	7	8	9	10

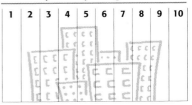

Common Health Problems

For experienced dog owners

BEAGLE

Height	13–16 in (33–40 cm)
Weight	26–33 lbs (12–15 kg)
Coat	short, smooth, very dense, not too fine
Color	all recognized hound colors (orange, white, black, tan, tricolor; always with white markings)

Grooming

1	2	3	4	5	6	7	8	9	10

Required Exercise

1	2	3	4	5	6	7	8	9	10

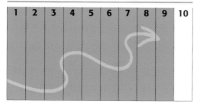

Suitability for City Living

1	2	3	4	5	6	7	8	9	10

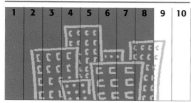

Common Health Problems

heart disease, epilepsy

Suitable for first-time owners

The **BEAGLE** is one of the oldest hound breeds. References to it can be found going back to the fourteenth century. It was used primarily for hunting rabbits and hares, working sometimes in packs and sometimes with hunters following on foot. The Beagle has an excellent nose, and that is the cause of its only fault as a family dog. Once it has found an interesting trail (a rabbit, a rat, a neighbor on the way to the corner store), that very fine nose is glued to the ground, and the dog is gone. No weather is bad enough to stop the Beagle, no distance too great to discourage it. No other dog is braver or more persistent than this little hound. It is not aggressive toward strangers, but does announce their arrival with a penetrating Beagle howl. The Beagle is calm, loyal, and friendly. Because there is not a trace of aggressiveness in its character, it is ideal for families with children. This is a loving, cheerful, and playful dog that adapts to just about any situation, but its feelings are easily hurt and it carries grudges. The hardest thing for the Beagle to learn is to come when called. The reason for this is that the hunting instinct of this dog is still so very strong. Also, a Beagle owner should know that the Beagle loves to eat. Not only does the size of its meals have to be carefully watched, but you also have to make sure your dog doesn't visit the compost heap in your garden, or your neighbor's garbage.

Height	20–22 in (50–56 cm)
Weight	approximately 66 lbs (30 kg)
Coat	dense double coat with soft undercoat and flat, hard, and shaggy guard hair
Color	blue, fawn, all shades of gray, black, or sandy; white only as a blaze on the face and on the tip of the tail, the top of the head, the chest, the neck, and the legs and feet

Grooming

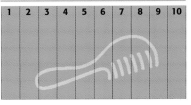

1	2	3	4	5	6	7	8	9	10

Required Exercise

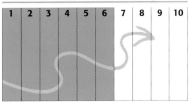

1	2	3	4	5	6	7	8	9	10

Suitability for City Living

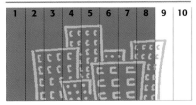

1	2	3	4	5	6	7	8	9	10

The **BEARDED COLLIE** was once a swift, agile, and adept herding dog used by Scottish shepherds and drovers in the seventeenth century. But that was long ago; in the meantime, the Bearded Collie has gained international fame as an elegant show dog. However, the great intelligence of the breed has not been affected by popularity and the emphasis on beauty. The Bearded Collie is an active, playful dog, easy to handle, adaptable, and always in good spirits. It has a great sense of humor that manifests itself in the outrageous things it does to avoid obeying a command. This dog needs a lot of exercise and plenty to keep it busy so that it will not get bored. If the Beardie is not played with enough, it starts to dig holes, yowl, jump over fences, or chew on things. Its ideal owner is someone who likes to jog or ride the bicycle. In spite of its career as a show dog, the Beardie has not lost its herding instinct, and it will keep trying to gather its people together like a flock of sheep. The Bearded Collie needs consistent and fair obedience training administered in a playful spirit; harsh discipline is out of place with this sensitive dog. The coat requires a lot of grooming, but offers excellent protection in bad weather, which is why the Beardie is always eager to be outside, no matter how cold or wet or windy it may be—often much more eager than its master.

Common Health Problems

hip dysplasia

Suitable for first-time owners

BEDLINGTON TERRIER

Height	15–16 in (38–40 cm)
Weight	18–22 lbs (8–10 kg)
Coat	thick, dense, and cottony
Color	blue, sandy, blue and tan, sandy and tan, liver and tan

Grooming

1	2	3	4	5	6	7	8	9	10

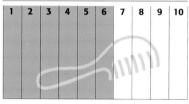

Required Exercise

1	2	3	4	5	6	7	8	9	10

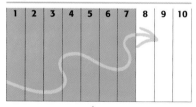

Suitability for City Living

1	2	3	4	5	6	7	8	9	10

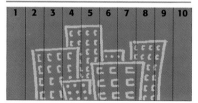

Common Health Problems

copper toxicosis, thyroid problems

Suitable for first-time owners

The **BEDLINGTON TERRIER** looks like a lamb, and this appearance can prove deceptive to the unwary. The breed was developed in England to hunt and kill rodents and other vermin, and it still responds with ruthless vigor to challengers or prey, an important fact for anyone contemplating getting a Bedlington. In outward appearance the Bedlington resembles no other terrier. It no doubt got its elegant lines and easy gait from the Whippet, from whom it also inherited its great speed. This dog is pleasant and quiet indoors, needs a lot of outdoor activity, but, if given enough exercise, adapts very well to family life and is much less temperamental than most terriers. It can be jealous of children and other pets, and it is therefore best for an older couple who have no grandchildren, but like to hike or bicycle and want a devoted friend and good watchdog. The Bedlington barks a lot and can be quite unfriendly toward strangers. Some Bedlingtons are timid or nervous, and it is therefore important that puppies be socialized early and exposed to many different sounds and noises. The coat should be professionally groomed. The Bedlington is truly a unique-looking animal, full of fire, individualism, and devotion—a fascinating dog for the right people.

Tervuren

Height	male: approximately 24 in (62 cm); female: 23 in (58 cm)
Weight	male: 59–70 lbs (27–32 kg); female: 50–55 lbs (22.5–25 kg)
Coat	long, smooth, double-coated
Color	mahogany to beige and gray, with black mask and black guard hairs

The **BELGIAN SHEEPDOG** is a rascal and prankster, ready to play until it drops of exhaustion, and it keeps this spirit up into old age. Anyone who fails to appreciate this quality had better look for another type of sheepdog because all Belgians are alike in this respect. The different varieties are anatomically all the same; they simply wear different clothing, so to speak. They are all lively, agile, intelligent, obedient, and rugged. The Malinois has become slightly more aggressive since dog enthusiasts discovered it a few years back. Belgian Sheepdogs are watchful and protective by nature; they love to be given tasks and are extremely competent agility and rescue dogs. They become completely attached to their people and need their proximity and affection. Because of their sensitivity, these dogs should never be owned by people of a despotic or temperamental disposition. The Belgian Sheepdog does not like being yelled at and has an elephant's memory, it will never forget a negative experience. It finds children irresistible, and some owners claim they never had a better babysitter for their kids. But the breed has a long adolescent phase and should not be trained seriously too early, even though the dogs may seem eager to learn. The Belgian is so dependent on its people that it will adjust to any living arrangement. You could share a telephone booth with this dog, as long as you give it enough opportunity to work off its excess energy. *Note:* Three types of Belgian Sheepdog are featured on the next page.

Grooming

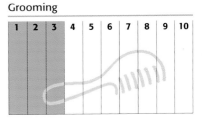

1	2	3	4	5	6	7	8	9	10

Required Exercise

1	2	3	4	5	6	7	8	9	10

Suitability for City Living

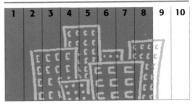

1	2	3	4	5	6	7	8	9	10

Common Health Problems

Suitable for first-time owners

Groenendael

Height	male: approximately 24 in (62 cm); female: 23 in (58 cm)
Weight	male: 59–70 lbs (27–32 kg); female: 50–55 lbs (22.5–25 kg)
Coat	long, smooth, double-coated
Color	black, some white permitted

Malinois

Height	male: approximately 24 in (62 cm); female: 23 in (58 cm)
Weight	male: 59–70 lbs (27–32 kg); female: 50–55 lbs (22.5–25 kg)
Coat	short, dense, double-coated
Color	red to fawn, with black mask

Laekenois

Height	male: approximately 24 in (62 cm); female: 23 in (58 cm)
Weight	male: 59–70 lbs (27–32 kg); female: 50–55 lbs (22.5–25 kg)
Coat	rough, shaggy, hairs approximately 2 in long
Color	dun, with traces of soot on muzzle and tail; a little white is tolerated

Height	male: 25–28 in (64–70 cm) female: 23–26 in (58–66 cm)
Weight	male: 79–106 lbs (36–48 kg) female: 75–90 lbs (34–41 kg)
Coat	long, luxurious, shiny
Color	jet black with rich rust-colored markings on cheeks, over the eyes, on sides of chest, and on all four legs; symmetrical white blaze and white markings on chest, tip of tail, and all four feet

In earlier times, the **BERNESE MOUNTAIN DOG** was the working dog of Swiss farmers, pulling carts with vats of milk to market and guarding the homestead. In the course of the nineteenth century, the breed almost died out. But since its picture was prominently displayed in advertisements for a brand of dry dog food in the 1970s, the Bernese Mountain Dog has become almost as fashionable as the West Highland White Terrier. It is, in fact, a very pleasant companion dog: handsome, gentle, friendly, and affectionate. If it has any fault at all, it is a tendency to be a one-man dog. The Bernese Mountain Dog needs a lot of exercise and suffers from the heat, and is therefore recommended for city living only with reservations. Nevertheless, this dog is often seen in big-city parks and is very popular with urban dwellers who own sport utility vehicles. The Bernese needs space, preferably a yard it can guard and to which it can retreat when it gets too hot indoors. Obedience training should be started early and kept up. This dog is simply too large and powerful for disobedience to be tolerated. Vigilant by nature and somewhat aggressive, the Bernese should never be trained as a guard dog; its size and deep voice are enough to keep intruders away. It is important to purchase a Bernese from someone who has been breeding these dogs since before the boom started, preferably for 15 or 20 years.

Grooming

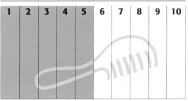

1	2	3	4	5	6	7	8	9	10

Required Exercise

1	2	3	4	5	6	7	8	9	10

Suitability for City Living

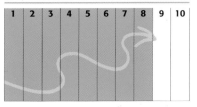

1	2	3	4	5	6	7	8	9	10

Common Health Problems

hip dysplasia, sometimes twisted stomach

Suitable for first-time owners

BICHON FRISÉ

Height	9–11 in (24–29 cm)
Weight	7–13 lbs (3–6 kg)
Coat	soft, thick undercoat beneath coarser, somewhat curly guard hairs
Color	pure white

Grooming

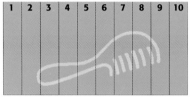

Required Exercise

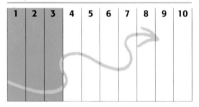

Suitability for City Living

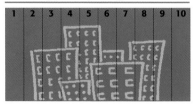

Common Health Problems

Suitable for first-time owners

The **BICHON FRISÉ** is a small French companion dog whose early history is not well known. It is probably descended from small spaniels, the Poodle, or the Maltese. Whatever its origins, the Bichon is a charming little companion dog, and this is the only thing it is good for. It has a cheerful nature, is playful, affectionate, and lively, and is easy to live with. It barks very little, is always in good spirits, wants to be included in whatever is happening, and tries very hard to please. Its requirements for exercise are minimal, but taking care of its coat is a major job. This dog can look either like an exquisite white powder puff, or a matted mess of knotted fur—it all depends on the owner. The Bichon is sensitive and easy to teach. It adapts well to just about any situation, but can't deal with the rough handling small children tend to display toward pets.

Height	23–27 in (58–68 cm)
Weight	88–106 lbs (40–48 kg)
Coat	short and hard
Color	black and tan, bright red, liver with tan markings; small amounts of white on chest or feet are permitted

Grooming

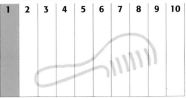

Required Exercise

Suitability for City Living

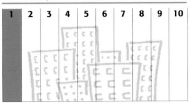

Common Health Problems

hip dysplasia, twisted stomach, entropion

For experienced dog owners

The **BLOODHOUND**, or **ST. HUBERT HOUND,** is the oldest of all the hounds that hunt by scent. Beagles, Bassets, and Spaniels all have Bloodhound blood in their veins. The breed has existed since long before the time of Christ. Its name does not reflect, as it might seem, a bloodthirsty nature, but arose instead from the care with which the breeding was pursued to maintain the purity of the breed. Bloodhounds were aristocrats among dogs, and ordinary people referred to them as "blooded hounds." Bloodhounds have never been used to attack humans; in fact, this dog is so good-natured that it is pointless to try and train it as a guard or police dog. It is instead a marvelous family and companion dog. It is also famous for its ability to find missing people. Bloodhounds do not hunt people, but follow their scent. That is what they are used for. Once the quarry is found, the Bloodhound wags its tails happily and is delighted with itself. The Bloodhound is a loving, gentle, and friendly family dog. It is not particularly adept at following commands because the nature of its job is to tell its owner where to go, rather than the other way around. Because these dogs are very powerful as well as obstinate, they need a strong and consistent master. But this gentle breed is very sensitive and should never be treated roughly, or physically disciplined. Bloodhounds slobber a great deal and need a lot of exercise. They also have a unique voice. The Bloodhound is not some ordinary dog to have around the house; it is a very special dog for people who can truly appreciate its wonderful qualities.

BORDER COLLIE

Height	male: 19–21 in (48–53 cm); female: 18–20 in (45–51 cm)
Weight	29–48 lbs (13–22 kg)
Coat	water-resistant, double-coated, moderately long; the English standard also accepts short-haired dogs
Color	normally black and white, but there are also a variety of other colors; white must never predominate

Grooming

1	2	3	4	5	6	7	8	9	10

Required Exercise

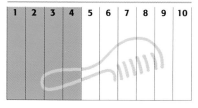

1	2	3	4	5	6	7	8	9	10

Suitability for City Living

1	2	3	4	5	6	7	8	9	10

Common Health Problems

retinal atrophy, hip dysplasia, epilepsy

For experienced dog owners

The **BORDER COLLIE** is very handsome and a fantastic herding dog of great strength, stamina, and speed. It is extremely intelligent, has an incredibly good eye, and is very active. When it does not have enough to do, it is like a tightly wound spring, ready to uncoil and burst into action if any opportunity presents itself. The Border Collie is said to have an even disposition and be lovable and easy to control. But this is the case only if its owner is an outdoors person who can keep the dog in a rural setting where it can roam and, above all, have plenty of work to do. If it is cooped up too much, the Border Collie becomes destructive, and will bark for hours on end. Left alone in the yard too long, it will manage to clear any fence, or make its way through any gate. Some Border Collies·even learn to turn handles. This dog is outstanding at agility trials, always trying to please its master. Since it is usually smarter than all the other dogs, it generally performs tasks and solves problems better and faster than its competitors.

If given enough to do, the Border Collie is a great family dog who protects its people. But it should be kept only by someone who is committed to this dog and offers it the kind of exercise, attention, activity, and subordination training that it needs and deserves.

Height	approximately 13 in (33 cm)
Weight	13–15 lbs (6–7 kg)
Coat	hard, dense, with thick undercoat hugging the body
Color	red, wheat, gray, tan, blue

The **BORDER TERRIER** is somewhat calmer, milder-tempered, and more obedient than most terriers, but it is still a very tough and tenacious dog. It originated in the border area between England and Scotland, and was used to drive out or kill foxes and other animals that might prey on lambs. The Border Terrier is very alert and active, unaffected by the elements, and able to follow horseback riders for hours. At the same time it is so adaptable that it willingly accepts any living situation, as long as it has enough human company and gets taken on long walks. The Border Terrier is very attached to its people and is very intelligent, and it therefore responds well to training. But it is a true terrier, and blind obedience is not to be expected of this type of dog. The Border Terrier has a strong mind of its own, a pronounced hunting instinct, and a very active temperament. Consequently, a badly raised Border Terrier can make life miserable for everybody around it. However, it is also eager to please and very sensitive. If obedience training is started early enough, this dog should present no problems. The Border Terrier also gets along with children and other dogs if it gets used to them at an early age.

Grooming

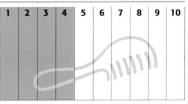

| 1 | 2 | 3 | 4 | 5 | 6 | 7 | 8 | 9 | 10 |

Required Exercise

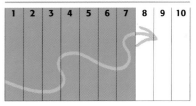

| 1 | 2 | 3 | 4 | 5 | 6 | 7 | 8 | 9 | 10 |

Suitability for City Living

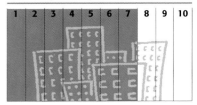

| 1 | 2 | 3 | 4 | 5 | 6 | 7 | 8 | 9 | 10 |

Common Health Problems

Suitable for first-time owners

BORZOI

Height	26–32 in (65–82 cm)
Weight	78–106 lbs (35–48 kg)
Coat	long, wavy, very thick, double-coated
Color	white, gold, tan, black-ticked, gray, brindle

Grooming

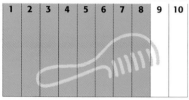

Required Exercise

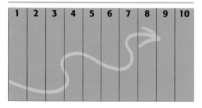

Suitability for City Living

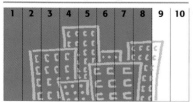

Common Health Problems

crowded canine teeth

For experienced dog owners

The **BORZOI** is a true aristocrat among dogs. Bred in Russia for hunting wolves, it is now appreciated above all for its distinguished looks and for a beauty of movements surpassed by no other breed. It runs like a dream, as though floating across the ground. Indoors, the Borzoi is peaceful and quiet, but outdoors it turns into a determined and deadly predator if it sees an animal it considers prey. This should always be kept in mind, especially if there are other dogs nearby. A fighting Borzoi is a sight to strike terror into anyone's heart, not just because of its size and strength but also because of its lightning speed.

Ordinarily the Borzoi takes little interest in other dogs—or other people for that matter, except for its family. Though "arrogant" may seem like an anthropomorphizing term, it is altogether appropriate for this dog. The Borzoi is a one-man dog that accepts the existence of its master's family but barely takes cognizance of anyone else.

Height	14–15 in (36–38 cm)
Weight	14–24 lbs (6.5–11.3 kg)
Coat	short, smooth, and glossy
Color	black brindle with white markings

The **BOSTON TERRIER** is an American product and goes back to the mid-nineteenth century. The breed is the result of crossing the Pit Bull Terrier, the Bull Terrier, the Boxer, and the English Bulldog. However, the modern-day Boston Terrier has little in common with its ferocious ancestors. It is a friendly, lively companion dog of great charm and feels much more at home in an apartment, or on the show bench, than in the fighting ring. The breed standard states that the shape of the Boston Terrier's skull "indicates a high degree of intelligence," and this statement is more than a physical description. The Boston Terrier is very, very smart and likes nothing better than to learn new tricks. It is also a little powerhouse and very active, a combination than can either make for a marvelous companion or result in catastrophe because very few people know how to deal with a dog that is smarter than they are. Early socializing and obedience training, as well as regular exercise, are crucial for this dog to develop good manners. But a well-behaved Boston Terrier is a wonderful dog around children, as well as adults; it is clean, hardly smells at all, doesn't shed, and is vigilant without barking too much.

Grooming

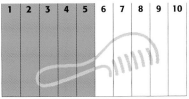

| 1 | 2 | 3 | 4 | 5 | 6 | 7 | 8 | 9 | 10 |

Required Exercise

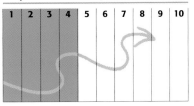

| 1 | 2 | 3 | 4 | 5 | 6 | 7 | 8 | 9 | 10 |

Suitability for City Living

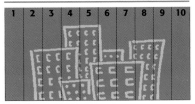

| 1 | 2 | 3 | 4 | 5 | 6 | 7 | 8 | 9 | 10 |

Common Health Problems

tends to be short-winded, allergies

Suitable for first-time owners

BOUVIER DES FLANDRES

Height	male: 28 in (70 cm); female: 26 in (67 cm)
Weight	75–95 lbs (34–43 kg)
Coat	shaggy
Color	black or gray, dun, salt-and-pepper brindle

Grooming

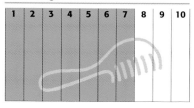

1	2	3	4	5	6	7	8	9	10

Required Exercise

1	2	3	4	5	6	7	8	9	10

Suitability for City Living

1	2	3	4	5	6	7	8	9	10

Common Health Problems

twisted stomach, hip dysplasia

For experienced dog owners

Cattle driving was the **BOUVIER DES FLANDRES**'s original job in Belgium, and it apparently still thinks only work keeps a body in shape. That is why it needs plenty of space and exercise, and is best kept in a rural environment. The Bouvier loves to be close to people, and anyone who does not like the idea of a permanent and massive foot warmer should look for a different dog. Yet the Bouvier is not so much a one-man dog as a family pet. It is good with children and very vigilant without being a yapper. It barks only if there is a good reason for it. The Bouvier looks like a big bear, but is very agile and athletic. Courageous and protective, it is reserved toward strangers, but adores its family. Because it is also very territorial, it has to obey commands with absolute reliability. This requires strict training, which must, however, be based on positive reinforcement. Yelling and yanking are completely counter-productive. Bouviers are very sensitive, and if they are treated unjustly they will hold it against you for a long time.

Owning a Bouvier des Flandres requires some special character qualities: You have to be patient and consistent. If you prize cleanliness above all else, you should also look for another kind of dog because Bouviers are big and very hairy, with paws that seem to pick up all the trash of the neighborhood and carry it into the house. But if you can put up with these inconveniences and are willing to take the time to train your dog, socialize it, and invest in its friendship, you will be rewarded with an irresistibly loyal companion and a fearless defender of the family.

Height	21–25 in (53–63 cm)
Weight	male: 66–70 lbs (30–32 kg); female: 53–55 lbs (24–25 kg)
Coat	short, flat, dense, glossy
Color	red, yellow, or brindle; with or without white markings

The **BOXER** was developed in Munich around 1850 through crossings of various Molossus-like dogs like the Bullenbeisser (a German bulldog) and the English Bulldog. The breed was originally used for fighting bulls and bears, but today the Boxer is a delightful people dog. Even the original, rather alarming facial expression has softened. The modern Boxer is a gentleman and an ideal family dog: loving, alert, and sweet-tempered, eager to participate in all activities, and intent on pleasing its master. It is great with children, patiently putting up with just about anything, from having food stuffed up its nose to being clung to by toddlers learning to walk. The Boxer is sometimes described as an "honest" dog because its face reveals its feelings so clearly. It is naturally suspicious of strangers, but is never unpredictable or deceitful. It needs long and regular walks to work off its energy, but can easily be kept in the city. It is very strong, active, and curious, and therefore has to be taught firmly, calmly, and consistently from puppyhood to obey. Otherwise, this dog will want to take charge of the couch, the bed, or even the kitchen table.

Grooming

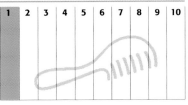

| 1 | 2 | 3 | 4 | 5 | 6 | 7 | 8 | 9 | 10 |

Required Exercise

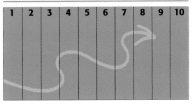

| 1 | 2 | 3 | 4 | 5 | 6 | 7 | 8 | 9 | 10 |

Suitability for City Living

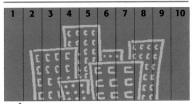

| 1 | 2 | 3 | 4 | 5 | 6 | 7 | 8 | 9 | 10 |

Common Health Problems

hip dysplasia, tumors, heart disease, progressive axonopathy, spondylitis

Suitable for first-time owners

BRIARD

Height	male: 24–27 in (62–68 cm); female: 22–29 in (56–64 cm)
Weight	approximately 66 lbs (30 kg)
Coat	long, shaggy, slightly wavy, with thick undercoat
Color	fawn, black, gray

Grooming

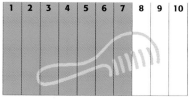

| 1 | 2 | 3 | 4 | 5 | 6 | 7 | 8 | 9 | 10 |

Required Exercise

| 1 | 2 | 3 | 4 | 5 | 6 | 7 | 8 | 9 | 10 |

Suitability for City Living

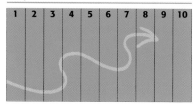

| 1 | 2 | 3 | 4 | 5 | 6 | 7 | 8 | 9 | 10 |

The **BRIARD** is probably the oldest French herding dog. Its job was to defend sheep against thieves and feral dogs. Because the Briard has an exceptionally fine sense of hearing, it was used in World War I as a sentry dog. Stories of its heroism abound, and the Briard is, in fact, exceptionally courageous, loyal, obedient, and generous-spirited. However, it is not a dog for people to whom a hygienically clean house matters above all else—the coat has to be groomed regularly because it gets matted very quickly—or for people who hope that training will show instant results. The Briard learns slowly, but what it has once learned, it retains for life. It is a good athlete, agile and energetic, that uses its head and needs an owner who is at least as smart as it is. An extremely vigilant dog, it is suspicious of strangers and watches them carefully, even after it has known them for some time. The Briard needs a lot of exercise. Accompanying someone on a bicycle for an hour or two is an ideal outing once the dog is at least one year old. It does not like to obey people whose leadership qualities it doubts, even though it is basically well-behaved and cooperative. The Briard seldom roams because it prefers staying near its master to be able to defend him or her should the need arise.

Common Health Problems

hip dysplasia, progressive atrophy of the retina

For experienced dog owners

Height	24–27 in (61–68.5 cm)
Weight	88–110 lbs (40–50 kg)
Coat	short, hard, smooth
Color	red, fawn, brindle

Grooming

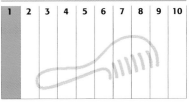

Required Exercise

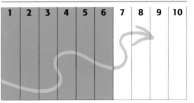

Suitability for City Living

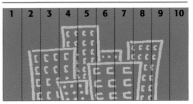

Common Health Problems

hip dysplasia, tumors, eyelid abnormalities, twisted stomach, dermatitis, tendency to develop eczema

For experienced dog owners

The **BULL MASTIFF** is, as its name implies, a cross between the Mastiff and the Bulldog. It was developed toward the end of the last century to help English gamekeepers defend against poachers. The dog's job was to track down poachers, throw them, and hold them without biting until the gamekeeper could catch up and arrest them. Today's Bull Mastiff, though not a dog to challenge thoughtlessly, is normally docile. It no longer inspires the kind of fear poachers must have felt in earlier times. (In those days poachers had the unfortunate habit of shooting gamekeepers rather than risk arrest, which is why the need for a dog like this arose.) The Bull Mastiff slobbers; it is usually mild-mannered and easy to handle, but takes its tasks very seriously. Once its instinct to protect has been aroused, it is very hard to convince it to relax. The Bull Mastiff belongs in a rural environment, but could be kept in the city if it can get enough exercise. Though very obstinate and incredibly strong, it responds well to early, firm, and prolonged training. The Bull Mastiff is absolutely fearless and should never to be trained as a guard dog, nor should the slightest evidence of aggression toward people be tolerated. With as big and strong a dog as this, such a tendency could have disastrous consequences. The dog's looks alone are enough to scare away any intruder.

BULL TERRIER

Height	the standard does not prescribe any specific height
Weight	55–70 lbs (25–32 kg)
Coat	hard, short, thin, shiny
Color	pure white, white with markings, fawn, red, brindle, tricolor; colored dogs may have white markings

Grooming

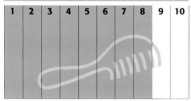

| 1 | 2 | 3 | 4 | 5 | 6 | 7 | 8 | 9 | 10 |

Required Exercise

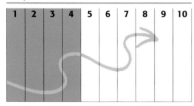

| 1 | 2 | 3 | 4 | 5 | 6 | 7 | 8 | 9 | 10 |

Suitability for City Living

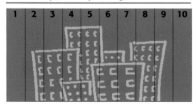

| 1 | 2 | 3 | 4 | 5 | 6 | 7 | 8 | 9 | 10 |

Common Health Problems

heart disease, kidney problems, occasional deafness in white dogs

For experienced dog owners

At one time a ferocious fighter, the **BULL TERRIER** was bred around 1830 by crossing the English Bulldog with the old, now extinct, white English Terrier. The aim was to get a lighter, more agile fighting dog. By now it has become a polite and obedient dog, with an irresistible sense of humor. It is loyal, affectionate, and loving. But it gets bored easily and cannot, therefore, be acquired and then ignored. Because this is a very strong-willed and powerful dog, it is not a good choice for someone who is not assertive, or has never owned a dog. At the same time, the Bull Terrier is playful and silly and can easily be kept in the city if it is allowed to be part of the family, and if it is offered enough walks and adventure. The ideal owners would be a family that loves horseplay, racing, and games like frisbee marathons. The Bull Terrier has the potential to become a first-class companion dog, but in the wrong hands it can turn out to be a horrid disaster. This breed is, by the way, very sensitive to cold and dampness, and loves to be warm and comfortable.

Height	12 in (30 cm)
Weight	13 lbs (6 kg)
Coat	hard and waterproof, with a thick undercoat; has to be trimmed regularly
Color	red, sand, from light gray to almost black, brindle; white is a fault

Grooming

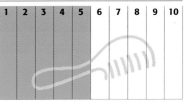

1	2	3	4	5	6	7	8	9	10

Required Exercise

1	2	3	4	5	6	7	8	9	10

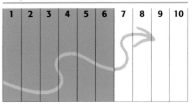

Suitability for City Living

1	2	3	4	5	6	7	8	9	10

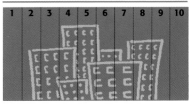

Common Health Problems

dislocation of kneecap

Suitable for first-time owners

The **CAIRN TERRIER** is a Scottish working terrier: tough, fearless, and independent. This is not the dog for someone who insists on absolute obedience. The breed was raised for centuries to get rid of nuisance animals, and it was left up to the dog to decide whether to kill its prey in the burrow or drag it out alive. But someone who likes the idea of having a dog that thinks for itself will have fun with the Cairn Terrier. It is the ideal dog for people with a sense of humor. If a Cairn performs a certain trick on one day, you can be sure it won't repeat it when you ask it the next day. But wait until next week, and it may perform it again all on its own.

The Cairn Terrier loves excitement and adventure and is therefore wrong for people who want a dog to walk around the block with once a day. It is very intelligent and can't be left to entertain itself in the yard. Cairns expect a lot of attention and entertainment from their people, and will repay their owners a hundredfold for their time and effort. A well-trained Cairn Terrier is almost like a small, independent-minded person who knows what you want of him before he is even asked. The United States Air Force has used Cairn Terriers as search dogs for illegal drugs because they can get into places too tight for the larger German Shepherds. The Cairn Terrier has complete self-confidence and will undertake just about anything it can think of, simply because nobody ever told it there might be some things beyond its powers and capabilities.

CARDIGAN WELSH CORGI

Height	12 in (30 cm)
Weight	28–30 lbs (12.7–13.6 kg)
Coat	short, dense, weather-resistant
Color	red, brown, black, tricolor, blue merle

Grooming

1	2	3	4	5	6	7	8	9	10

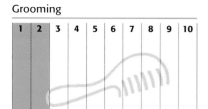

Required Exercise

1	2	3	4	5	6	7	8	9	10

Suitability for City Living

1	2	3	4	5	6	7	8	9	10

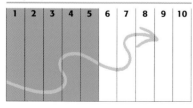

Common Health Problems

Suitable for first-time owners

The **CARDIGAN WELSH CORGI** is a very old breed. It is believed to have been brought to Wales by the Celtic people around the year 1200 and to have sprung from the same progenitors that produced the Dachshund. It was an all-purpose dog, used for herding small farm animals, guarding the homestead, driving the neighbor's cattle away, and catching and killing rats and other marauding animals. This small dog has enough spunk and enthusiasm to do almost any task it is set, and it is smart enough to learn just about anything. Unlike the Pembroke Welsh Corgi, the Cardigan—"the Corgi with the tail"—is an incredibly tough dog and a terrifying adversary to animals it attacks. It doesn't know fear and moves with lightning speed despite its short legs. Because it is also quite vigilant and territorial, there can be unpleasant encounters. That is why it is important to train a Cardigan Corgi well, and to start early. Cardigans are long-lived and keep having to be reminded of the lessons they have learned. But they also have a real need to please their masters and will adjust to whatever is going on around them. Cardigans are reserved with strangers and perhaps a little too suspicious, and it is therefore advisable to make it clear to them that watchfulness is appreciated, but nothing more than barking is required. Cardigans tend to be one-person dogs, but the person who has won this dog's friendship will enjoy a loyalty that is unmatched. The love of a Cardigan Welsh Corgi is a rare privilege.

Height	10–13 in (25–34 cm)
Weight	10–19 lbs (4.4–8.8 kg)
Coat	soft, silky, long, with abundant feathering
Color	black with tan markings (black and tan), ruby, tricolor (Prince Charles), and white with chestnut or yellowish red patches (Blenheim)

Grooming

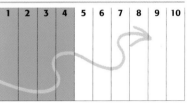

Required Exercise

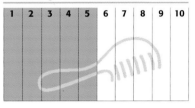

Suitability for City Living

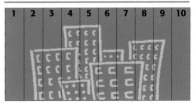

The **CAVALIER KING CHARLES SPANIEL** has been a favorite of the highest society of England ever since the sixteenth century when the breed was developed. King Charles II kept a whole pack of these pretty little spaniels and is said to have spent more time playing with his dogs than tending to the affairs of state.

A close relative of the King Charles Spaniel, the Cavalier King Charles makes its appearance in many portraits of high-ranking ladies by Rubens, Rembrandt, and Gainsborough. This is not surprising since this dog combines the virtues of a lap dog—toy size and a real interest in the social activities of a salon—with those of a sporting breed. It loves to go on walks and has an excellent nose. The latter can cause it to manifest a hunting spirit that is quite amazing to see in a luxury dog.

The Cavalier King Charles Spaniel is an ideal family dog, easy to keep entertained and to teach, always in good spirits, polite and playful, loving and friendly, and easy to handle even for children. It finds all humans delightful and likes to express this feeling with loud enthusiasm.

Common Health Problems

heart disease, hip dysplasia, eye problems such as cataracts and retinal atrophy

Suitable for first-time owners

CHESAPEAKE BAY RETRIEVER

Height	male: 23–26 in (58–66 cm); female: 21–24 in (53–61 cm)
Weight	male: 66–84 lbs (30–38 kg); female: 55–70 lbs (25–32 kg)
Coat	coarse, hard, oily; with short, soft undercoat; wavy
Color	"deadgrass" (the term is self-explanatory) or any shade of brown

Grooming

1	2	3	4	5	6	7	8	9	10

Required Exercise

1	2	3	4	5	6	7	8	9	10

Suitability for City Living

1	2	3	4	5	6	7	8	9	10

The **CHESAPEAKE BAY RETRIEVER** is the toughest and strongest of all the retrievers. Developed about one hundred years ago in Maryland, it was unsurpassed for hunting water fowl, often retrieving a hundred or more ducks a day in the worst weather, disregarding cold and icy water, and enjoying every minute of it. It is, to this day, by far the best retriever of ducks and should be kept only by people who use it for hunting. At the same time, however, it very much needs human companionship and is a devoted family dog that loves children. It is loyal, intelligent, of a happy disposition, watchful, and always eager to please its master. But the very qualities that make it such a superb retriever—tremendous willpower, physical strength, single-minded concentration on the hunt—can easily be misread as unruly obstinacy in a dog that is kept purely as a family dog. The Chesapeake has to be able to recognize its place in the hierarchy of the household. Anyone who owns this dog has to train it with love, but also with a firm hand and consistency, in order to earn its respect. This training has to start while the dog is still a puppy to prevent the Chesapeake from developing into an obstinate or aggressive adult dog.

Common Health Problems

hip dysplasia, eczema

For experienced dog owners

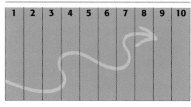

Height	approximately 5 in (13 cm)
Weight	1–6 lbs (.5–2.5 kg)
Coat	short-haired variety: smooth, dense, short, close to the body, and glossy; long-haired variety: soft, fringed
Color	all colors permitted

Grooming

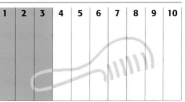

Required Exercise

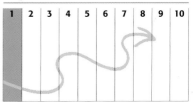

Suitability for City Living

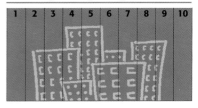

The **CHIHUAHUA** is the world's smallest dog and the ultimate apartment dog. It probably originated in Mexico. The long-haired variety was developed later on in the United States. The Chihuahua is the perfect dog for older people or those living in small apartments. It hates the cold and the damp, and therefore does not have to be taken outside much. But it is desperately unhappy if it is left out of any activity. The Chihuahua has a spot on the back of its head where the bones of the skull are not entirely fused; this fontanel always has to be protected—a blow to it could kill the dog.

A Chihuahua needs close contact with its people and loves everybody it knows. It tends to have delusions of grandeur and is a noisy, furious watchdog. It also approaches other dogs with the self-confidence of a Newfoundland. Because of this, it has to be watched closely since it would not have a chance if it really got into a fight. The Chihuahua is sometimes given to fits of temper and can be a fussy eater. If it is overprotected and babied too much, it will often become timid and insecure and snap at people—better to leave it to its illusions of being a Newfoundland! All in all, the Chihuahua is a little tyrant that turns its owners into its slaves. But that is exactly its purpose in life: to exist purely and solely to be loved and spoiled.

Common Health Problems

back problems, fractures (don't let dog jump off furniture), dislocated jaw, rheumatism, heart disease, diabetes, dislocation of kneecap, epilepsy

Suitable for first-time owners

CHINESE CRESTED

Height	male: 12–13 in (30–33 cm); female: 9–12 in (23–30 cm)
Weight	up to 12 lbs (5.5 kg)
Coat	hairless variety: long, soft tufts of hair on top of head and on paws and tail; powderpuff variety: soft, silky, abundant
Color	all colors and color combinations

Grooming

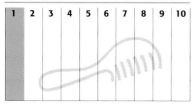

Required Exercise

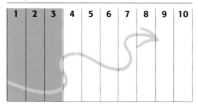

Suitability for City Living

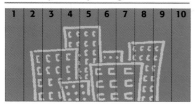

Common Health Problems

bad teeth; the hairless variety tends to have dry skin

Suitable for first-time owners

The **CHINESE CRESTED** can be traced back in China to the thirteenth century, but did not appear in Europe until the mid-1800s. Whether of the hairless or powderpuff variety, it is a graceful, spirited, cheerful, and intelligent luxury dog with lots of character. It loves its people tenderly and gets along beautifully with other dogs and pets. Though lively and playful, it is a perfect apartment dog because it is content to get most of the exercise it needs playing indoors with a ball. It is very smart and responds well to friendly training, which is essential if its great desire for activity is to be kept under control. Both varieties are quite hardy; however, the Chinese Hairless should be protected from wet and cold weather, though not pampered. Contrary to many stories, it does not necessarily get sunburned but tans nicely as long as it is not exposed to the hot sun too suddenly or too long. Nor does it die of cold in the winter, as long as it gets enough exercise when outside. If it is not treated like a fragile doll, this rare dog behaves with great self-confidence and shows a keen interest in everything that goes on around it.

Height	male: 19–22 in (48–55 cm); female: 18–20 in (45–50 cm)
Weight	55–62 lbs (25–28 kg)
Coat	a short-haired variety is very rare; the coat of the long-haired variety is very thick, abundant, soft, and standing away from the body; with a soft, wooly undercoat
Color	black, red, blue, cinnamon, and cream or white

Grooming

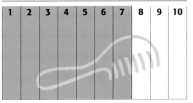

Required Exercise

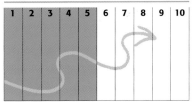

Suitability for City Living

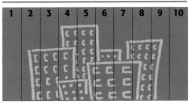

Common Health Problems

hip dysplasia, skin problems, entropion

For experienced dog owners

The first known pictorial representation of the **CHOW CHOW** is in a Chinese bas-relief from about 2,000 years ago. The name comes from the Cantonese word "chow," which means "food." This suggests that this dog was originally bred to add variety to people's menu—eating dog meat was a common custom in China. This history may possibly account for the Chow's aloofness. Chows are reserved and unfriendly, but always polite; they are not very affectionate and are reluctant to play. But the Chow Chow is totally devoted to the one person it recognizes as its master. It is not a good dog around children. Even if it learns to accept the children of its master, this does not mean that it will accept their friends. It is very important that this dog receive friendly obedience training and be well socialized because it is very strong, and can be aggressive toward other animals. The mass of fur—which requires considerable care—makes the Chow look larger than it is, and the folds of its face can make it appear dangerous. But dangerous it is not—obstinate and pig-headed, yes. It cannot be forced to do anything, but often can be talked into doing what you want it to do. Strangers should not expect to be greeted with a friendly wag of the tail. In fact, they should not expect anything at all from a Chow, as long as it does not perceive them as a threat to its people.

CLUMBER SPANIEL

Height	12–14 in (30–35 cm)
Weight	55–69 lbs (25–31.5 kg)
Coat	profuse, straight, silky
Color	pure white with lemon markings

Grooming

1	2	3	4	5	6	7	8	9	10

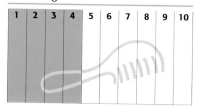

Required Exercise

1	2	3	4	5	6	7	8	9	10

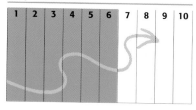

Suitability for City Living

1	2	3	4	5	6	7	8	9	10

The **CLUMBER SPANIEL** is the least spaniel-like of all the spaniels. Its history is quite mysterious. Named for the Clumber Estate in Nottingham, the breed is, however, believed to have originated in France. In the eighteenth century, the Clumber was the hunting companion of retired gentlemen out shooting pheasant and partridge. It is a solid-bodied, slow, and serious dog that exhibits amazing perseverence in the field, however. It has astonishing strength and is a fantastic and willing retriever, withstanding the worst weather and working conditions. Living with a Clumber Spaniel is somewhat like living with an elderly man, and it is therefore not everybody's choice of an ideal house dog. The Clumber is absolutely faithful to its master in a quiet, undemonstrative way, but can be very much a one-man dog and rather moody. It drools, snores, and wheezes somewhat. Anyone looking for a dog with social savoir-faire had better explore other breeds. The Clumber is not interested in anyone except its master. It has little inclination for play, but likes to follow as a quiet, somewhat lethargic companion. It is dignified, stoic, calm, absolutely professional in its work, and responds well to early, consistent, and firm training.

Common Health Problems

hip dysplasia

Suitable for first-time owners

Height	male: 24 in (60 cm); female: 22 in (55 cm)
Weight	48–70 lbs (22–32 kg)
Coat	long-haired or rough variety: long, straight, coarse guard hair with soft and very dense undercoat; short-haired or smooth variety: short, dense, lying close to the body
Color	sable with white, tricolor, or blue merle; all with white markings

Ever since the *Lassie* movies, the **COLLIE** has had an aura of the legendary. Everybody knows the Collie, knows it as the perfect dog that can do anything—probably even read and write. Originally an intelligent, reliable, and very useful working dog from the Scottish Highlands, the Collie suffered the consequence of huge popularity in the wake of its film success. Inexperienced dog owners bought it with utterly unrealistic expectations. It was supposed to be the ideal dog for children, the perfect babysitter, faithful unto death, and have an unerring sense for telling the good from the evil. The breed underwent a process of "improvement," becoming more and more elegant, a star at dog shows, while its character qualities suffered. Eventually the fad passed, and the breed was saved after even the most obtuse fan of the television series finally realized that the Collie was indeed exceptionally oriented and devoted to humans, but that it was still a dog and did not possess perfect manners. The Collie is headstrong, but also very sensitive. It has to be trained gently, but emphatically. It normally does not want anything to do with people it doesn't know and has to be socialized early in life to keep it from being timid with strangers as an adult dog. The Collie needs a lot of exercise and things to keep it busy (even the extremes of selective breeding have not succeeded in obliterating its work instinct), or else it can turn into a hyperactive barker.

Grooming

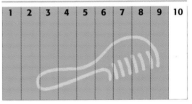

| 1 | 2 | 3 | 4 | 5 | 6 | 7 | 8 | 9 | 10 |

Required Exercise

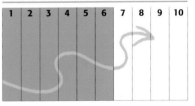

| 1 | 2 | 3 | 4 | 5 | 6 | 7 | 8 | 9 | 10 |

Suitability for City Living

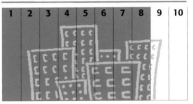

| 1 | 2 | 3 | 4 | 5 | 6 | 7 | 8 | 9 | 10 |

Common Health Problems

"Collie eye," deafness in merles

Suitable for first-time owners

COTON DE TULÉAR

Height	10–11 in (25–28 cm)
Weight	12–15 lbs (5.4–6.8 kg)
Coat	hair about 3 in long, fine, and slightly wavy
Color	white; small gray or lemon spots on the ears permitted

Grooming

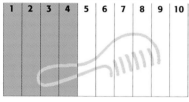

Required Exercise

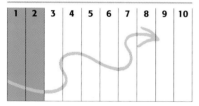

Suitability for City Living

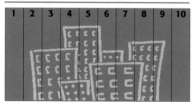

Common Health Problems

Suitable for first-time owners

The **COTON DE TULÉAR** probably has the same ancestors as the Maltese. During the colonial period of Madagascar, it was a favored pet of the French aristocrats living on the island, who did not allow ordinary people to own this dog. Times have changed, obviously, and ownership is no longer restricted to certain social classes. Moreover, these dogs are no longer as rare as they were just a few years ago. This is hardly surprising. The Coton is an ideal small family dog, spunky, with a sense of humor, eager to learn and easy to lead, attached to its people, and ready to adapt to just about any living situation. It is content to go for half an hour's walk, but can easily keep going for five hours. It can also be trained to become a fantastic agility dog. What matters to it above all else is to be included in all the family's activities. The Coton is extremely friendly and curious and is delighted by everything new. That is why it does not make a very good watchdog. If a thief should break into the house, the Coton would most likely think this was a wonderful change in the routine. It is healthy and vigorous and sheds relatively little. It needs no special grooming; just regular brushing will keep it looking elegant.

Height	male: 25–27 in (64–68.5 cm); female: 23–25 in (58–64 cm)
Weight	62–77 lbs (28–35 kg)
Coat	small, tight, very thick curls; water and dirt resistant
Color	black or liver

The **CURLY-COATED RETRIEVER** is a dog with very special working skills. There is hardly any other breed that exceeds it in retrieving game from the water. Australia and New Zealand are the places where this dog is most popular, whereas in Europe it is still quite unknown. This is not simply a Labrador or Golden Retriever with a curly coat. In fact, it is no good as an apartment or companion dog. The Curly-coated Retriever is an action dog ideal for hunting in marshy terrain and in any weather. It wants to, and has to, be able to swim, loves to feel the power of the wind, and enjoys being out in ice and snow under dark, threatening skies. Trying to create these conditions in your home is pretty near impossible, and walks in streets and parks are no acceptable substitute.

The Curly-coated Retriever is devoted to its master and family, but its friendliness does not extend to strangers. The most to be expected of it is aloof acceptance. This is a highly intelligent dog that does, however, like to use its intelligence to further its own ends, which is why early and thorough obedience training is important. But this very gentle and sensitive breed should never be treated roughly. The Curly-coated Retriever has a strong will of its own, but then without this quality it would not be the outstanding hunting dog it is.

Grooming

1	2	3	4	5	6	7	8	9	10

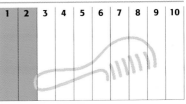

Required Exercise

1	2	3	4	5	6	7	8	9	10

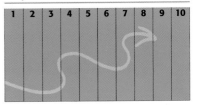

Suitability for City Living

1	2	3	4	5	6	7	8	9	10

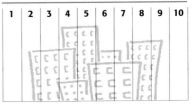

Common Health Problems

hip dysplasia, tumors

For experienced dog owners

DACHSHUND

Long-haired Dachshund

Size (chest circumference)	standard size: more than 14 in (35 cm); miniature size: 12–14 in (30–35 cm); toy size: up to 12 in (30 cm)
Weight	standard size: male, more than 15 lbs (7 kg); female, more than 14 lbs (6.5 kg); miniature size: male, up to 15 lbs (7 kg); female, less than 14 lbs (6.5 kg); toy size: male, up to 9 lbs (4 kg); female, up to 8 lbs (3.5 kg)
Coat	soft, sleek, shiny; well fringed on neck, ears, underside of body, legs, and tail
Color	solid red, golden red, yellow, also black and tan or tiger-striped

Grooming

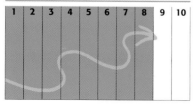

Required Exercise

Suitability for City Living

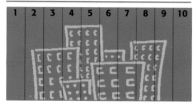

Common Health Problems

Dachshund paralysis, bladder stones

Suitable for first-time owners

The **DACHSHUND** is not a lap dog. Its name means "badger dog," and this describes the task for which it was bred. It is an outstanding hunter of animals in underground dens. Everyone knows Dachshunds have short, crooked legs, but there is a reason for these funny-looking legs: they are useful for digging fox, badgers, and rabbits out of their holes. People often make fun of Dachshunds, but this ridicule is far from deserved. After all, the dogs can't help loving too much or having too good an appetite. The Dachshund is a tough, courageous, and active dog, affectionate, clever, and without any complexes whatsoever. It is very self-confident and will not put up with any nonsense, which is why this dog should not be left unsupervised with children. The long-haired variety is said to be somewhat gentler and more docile than the smooth, and the wire-haired somewhat more aggressive and unpredictable. Dachshunds in general are extremely self-willed. There is hardly another breed that resists training as much as the Dachshund. It is extremely inventive in finding ways to avoid obeying commands, but if it is trained early, with quiet authority and patient persistence, the result will be a dog of great personality and originality. Anyone, however, who refuses to take this trouble may end up with a grumpy, astonishingly impolite dog. A pure-bred Dachshund that has learned to behave, on the other hand, is a treasure, endowed with a great sense of humor, amazing daring, and absolute loyalty.

Short-haired or Smooth

Size (chest circum- ference)	standard size: more than 14 in (35 cm); miniature size: 12–14 in (30–35 cm); toy size: up to 12 in (30 cm)
Weight	standard size: male, more than 15 lbs (7 kg); female, more than 14 lbs (6.5 kg); miniature size: male, up to 15 lbs (7 kg); female, up to 14 lbs (6.5 kg); toy size: male, up to 9 lbs (4 kg); female, up to 8 lbs (3.5 kg)
Coat	short, dense, shiny, lying close to the body
Color	solid red, golden-red, yellow; all with or without shading; also black and tan or tiger-striped

Wire-haired

Size (chest circum- ference)	standard size: more than 14 in (35 cm); miniature size: 12–14 in (30–35 cm); toy size: up to 12 in (30 cm)
Weight	standard size: male, more than 15 lbs (7 kg); female, more than 14 lbs (6.5 kg); miniature size: male, up to 15 lbs (7 kg); female, less than 14 lbs (6.5 kg); toy size: male, up to 9 lbs (4 kg); female, up to 8 lbs (3.5 kg)
Coat	dense, wiry, lying close to the body; interspersed with softer hair of undercoat
Color	red, wild boar, or badger color

DALMATIAN

Height	male: 22–24 in (55–60 cm); female: 21–23 in (54–59 cm)
Weight	male: 62–66 lbs (28–30 kg); female: 51 lbs (23 kg)
Coat	short, hard, dense, smooth, and glossy
Color	base color pure white, with black or liver spots of as uniform size as possible; puppies are pure white at birth

Grooming

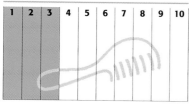

| 1 | 2 | 3 | 4 | 5 | 6 | 7 | 8 | 9 | 10 |

Required Exercise

| 1 | 2 | 3 | 4 | 5 | 6 | 7 | 8 | 9 | 10 |

Suitability for City Living

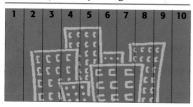

| 1 | 2 | 3 | 4 | 5 | 6 | 7 | 8 | 9 | 10 |

Common Health Problems

deafness, allergies (be careful with high-protein diets), bladder and kidney stones

Suitable for first-time owners

The **DALMATIAN** is a reliable, adaptable, happy, and playful companion dog with a sense of humor that borders on silliness. Much has been written in the last two hundred years about this breed's place of origin, but there is no agreement among authorities. The only indisputable fact is that the dog was first documented in Dalmatia in the former Yugoslavia, as its name suggests.

The Dalmatian has had many different jobs in its long career ranging from hound, shepherd, courier and retriever, "carriage dog," and guard dog of the homestead, to film star and family dog. Whatever is asked of it, the Dalmatian is delighted to do. It needs just two things to be happy: closeness to its master and enough physical activity. This breed was developed centuries ago to trot along next to a coach for 31 miles a day. "Enough physical activity" thus means a daily walk of several hours. Dalmatians are intelligent and curious, and when they are bored they get unhappy and destructive. Left alone in a yard or garden, they will remake the landscape according to their own notions, digging holes of astonishing size. Their activity level is comparable to that of a five-year-old after spending a rainy weekend indoors. Consequently, they make great playmates for children. They are watchful without barking too much. About 4 percent of Dalmatians are born deaf, and it is therefore advisable to buy from a breeder who routinely tests the hearing of the puppies.

Height	8–10 in (20–25 cm)
Weight	18 lbs (8 kg)
Coat	mixture of soft and hard hair about 2 in long
Color	pepper (silver to deep bluish black with silver topknot) or mustard (pale fawn to bright tan with cream-colored topknot)

Grooming

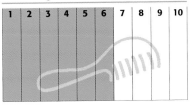

Required Exercise

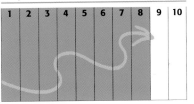

Suitability for City Living

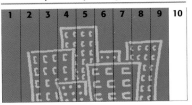

Common Health Problems

Suitable for first-time owners

The **DANDIE DINMONT TERRIER** is the only dog that is named after a character in a work of fiction. In Sir Walter Scott's novel *Guy Mannering*, a farmer named Dandie Dinmont has six small, rough-coated terriers who, thanks to the book's great popularity, became known as Dandie Dinmont Terriers. This is a little dog with a great personality—a fear-inspiring enemy of foxes and small predators, and usually a definite one-man dog. It is watchful without being a barker, reserved toward strangers, and generally without pity in dealing with other animals. Though self-assured, strong-willed, and with definite opinions of its own, it generally responds well to consistent and strict, but fair, training. The Dandie is a hardy dog and quite indifferent to pain. It therefore has to be watched closely. It is not uncommon for these dogs to be sick for days before giving any sign of not being well. If their coat is brushed enough and they have enough exercise, these dogs can be kept in the city as well as in the country.

DOBERMAN PINSCHER

Height	male: 27–28 in (68–72 cm); female: 25–27 in (63–68 cm)
Weight	66–88 lbs (30–40 kg)
Coat	short, hard, and dense, lying close to the body, glossy
Color	black, blue, or red; with sharply defined tan markings

Grooming

1	2	3	4	5	6	7	8	9	10

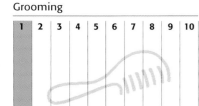

Required Exercise

1	2	3	4	5	6	7	8	9	10

Suitability for City Living

1	2	3	4	5	6	7	8	9	10

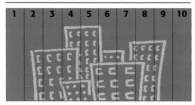

Common Health Problems

wobbler syndrome, heart disease

For experienced dog owners

The **DOBERMAN PINSCHER** is one of the few breeds about whose history there is no question. In 1860 a dog catcher named Louis Dobermann of Apolda, a town in Thuringia, Germany, set out to breed an aggressive, but absolutely obedient, dog to guard house and homestead. The result was a superb watchdog of noble and impressive appearance that was not to be trifled with. By now the Doberman has become a docile family dog that is easy to handle, but has lost none of its original protective instinct. It is an active dog that needs extensive walks to be happy and calm. This dog is surrounded by contradictory myths claiming, on the one hand, that it is a gentle, loving, and trustworthy pet and, on the other, that it is a born killer. The truth, as usual, lies somewhere in the middle. The Doberman can be very nervous. It is highly intelligent and easily trained if the owner knows what he or she is doing. But it can also be aggressive and very dangerous. This beautiful and loyal dog does not belong in the hands of a neophyte dog owner—it is much too much dog for such a person. The Doberman is very sensitive and takes its cues from the world it finds itself in: if surrounded by excitable people, it too is excitable, and if the owner is playful, the Doberman too will be playful. But it will not put up with being treated unjustly and must never be hit or beaten. Anyone who decides to get a Doberman and accepts the responsibility this decision entails will have a working dog with an extremely interesting personality.

Height	12–14 in (30–35 cm)
Weight	51–55 lbs (23–25 kg)
Coat	short, fine-textured, glossy
Color	all colors permitted except black and black-and-tan

The **ENGLISH BULLDOG** was bred in the early thirteenth century for bullfighting. This origin is responsible for the breed's name as well as for the dog's appearance. The short muzzle and wide lower jaw were needed for the dog to clamp itself to the bull's nose like a vise, and the nose had to be upturned so that the dog could still breathe while clinging to the bull. In spite of its disagreeable beginnings, the English Bulldog is today a friendly and lovable dog that adores its family, and is unsurpassed in its relations with children. The English Bulldog loves with the depth of its heart and never tires of doing things with its people. It also gets along well with other animals. But it loves to eat and is defensive of its food. It should, therefore, be fed separately from other pets. Playful and high-spirited as a puppy, the Bulldog grows up to be a calm and dignified adult, whose walks—which it asks for and needs—resemble a leisurely amble more than an energetic stepping out. The Bulldog is not for those who expect absolute obedience from their dog, though the claim that Bulldogs think more slowly than other dogs is not true. They just have to think everything over very thoroughly. The English Bulldog is not a watchdog that barks, but if there is any danger to the family, it suddenly develops unexpected speed and agility. The English Bulldog does drool, and it snores very loudly, which might put some people off. It also tends to swallow air, which can be most unpleasant in an unventilated room. Never leave this dog in a hot car; Bulldogs can't stand the heat.

Grooming

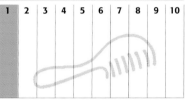

Required Exercise

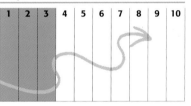

Suitability for City Living

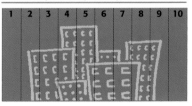

Common Health Problems

skin problems, respiratory problems, heart disease including heart attack, ectropion, entropion

Suitable for first-time owners

ENGLISH COCKER SPANIEL

Height	15–16 in (39.5–41 cm)
Weight	28–32 lbs (12.7–14.5 kg)
Coat	medium long, silky, flat, not wavy; legs, chest, and ears well feathered
Color	various colors permitted, such as red, white and orange, black, tan, and blue merle

Grooming

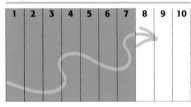

1	2	3	4	5	6	7	8	9	10

Required Exercise

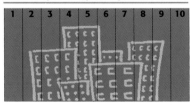

1	2	3	4	5	6	7	8	9	10

Suitability for City Living

1	2	3	4	5	6	7	8	9	10

Common Health Problems

Cocker madness in red dogs, ear problems, cataracts, retinal atrophy, kidney disease

The **ENGLISH COCKER SPANIEL** is an irresistible dog, which must be the reason why it is so popular. And its popularity is well deserved. Formerly used for hunting snipe, it is now kept primarily as a companion dog. Cheerful, lively, curious, and playful, it is also athletic and obedient. Its obedience is not an expression of subservience, but grows out of a genuine identification with its master's wishes. The Cocker has an excellent nose and loves to be on the go, tail constantly in motion. The ideal owner should be an active person who enjoys walking and hiking and gives the dog a chance to have some adventures. The Cocker has a wonderful sense of humor that borders on silliness, and it is always ready for any foolishness. Its marked sensibility makes it an interesting companion, one that is always intent on pleasing its master. It is easy to train, but should be taught with gentle persistence, never with impatience and anger. If left alone too much, this very energetic dog can easily develop some destructive habits. A good watchdog by nature, it has a tendency to bark too much, but normally the barking can be minimized with appropriate training.

Suitable for first-time owners

Height	male: 25–27 in (63–68.5 cm); female: 24–25 in (60–63 cm)
Weight	44–66 lbs (20–30 kg)
Coat	slightly wavy, long, and silky
Color	white with orange patches, black and white, white with black or blue patches, white and chestnut, tricolor (black, white, and tan)

Grooming

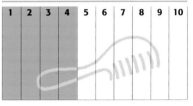

Required Exercise

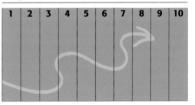

Suitability for City Living

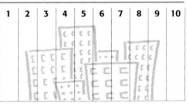

Common Health Problems

rare hip dysplasia

For experienced dog owners

The **ENGLISH SETTER** is the gentlest, as well as the fastest, of the three setter breeds. Though it looks handsome and elegant, it is definitely not meant to serve a decorative function in an apartment. It is, in fact one of the oldest pointer breeds, strong, tireless, and eager for action. At the same time, however, the English Setter is an incomparable family dog: loving and loyal, and patient and imperturbable with children. In return, it expects lots of love and attention from its people. It gets along fine with other animals, as well as with strangers. It does have a tendency to be headstrong and needs early and consistent training administered with patience and authority. Harshness is out of place with the English Setter. Like all setters, the English Setter is happiest if it can be very close to its people and is miserable if left alone all day.

Its pleasant nature and beauty have made the English Setter very popular, but anybody contemplating buying one of these dogs should keep in mind that they need a great deal of exercise and do not belong in the city. They must have daily walks of several hours as well as things to keep them occupied, neither of which is easy to provide in the city. Even the delightful, easy-going personality of the English Setter can change for the worse when the animal's basic needs are frustrated. This is obviously an elegant, breathtakingly beautiful animal, but it is just as obviously not an apartment dog.

ENGLISH SPRINGER SPANIEL

Height	20 in (50 cm)
Weight	48–53 lbs (22–24 kg)
Coat	moderately long, thick, flat, water- and weatherproof, silky, and glossy
Color	black and white, liver and white, reddish brown and white

Grooming

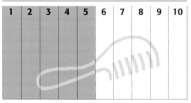

Required Exercise

Suitability for City Living

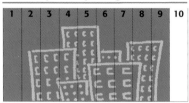

Common Health Problems

hip dysplasia, retinal atrophy, ear infections, allergies

Suitable for first-time owners

The **ENGLISH SPRINGER SPANIEL** is one of the few dogs that is just as nice as it looks. It is a loving, affectionate, good-tempered, and honest dog. A happy, playful, tail-wagging bundle of energy, it makes a great playmate for children. Although it adapts quite well to a quieter life in the city, the owner should not forget that the Springer Spaniel is still a good hunting dog, having the genes of one of the oldest English retrievers that was the progenitor of all English hunting spaniels. The English Springer loves water and retrieving, but its people are what it cares about more than anything else. This great attachment makes the English Springer easy to train. It should ideally have a yard to play in; if that is not feasible, it should at least be taken for long walks. Normally reserved with strangers, the English Springer can be trained to become a good watchdog. But left alone too much, it can easily develop some destructive habits.

Height	16–20 in (40–50 cm)
Weight	55–66 lbs (25–30 kg)
Coat	short, dense, hard, and glossy, lying close to the body
Color	black with yellow to fawn markings above the eyes and on cheeks and legs; also, regular white markings on head, throat, chest, and paws

Grooming

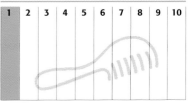

Required Exercise

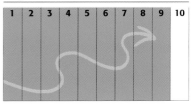

Suitability for City Living

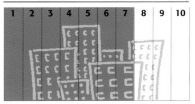

Common Health Problems

Suitable for first-time owners

The **ENTLEBUCHER SENNENHUND** comes from a plebeian background in the Entlebuch region in the canton of Lucerne in Switzerland. It was a farmer's dog and still enjoys a high reputation for its skills in managing herds of cows. An agile herding dog, it knows how to get away from the cattle, which it keeps nipping in the hock to make them move where they should.

The Entlebucher is very adaptable and can therefore, if necessary, be kept in the city as long as the owner makes sure it has enough exercise and things to keep it occupied. This dog is very energetic, as well as amusing, and highly intelligent. Left to itself, it will think up all kinds of trouble to get into, simply because it is bored. It is great with children if it has grown up around them, extremely patient and affectionate, and makes a wonderful baby-sitter that will courageously defend its charges if necessary. The Entlebucher is a good watchdog in general, and is very trainable if taught with fairness, consistency, and love. It delights in any kind of task or work, including subordination exercises. The Entlebucher Sennenhund is relatively rare but, as in the case of other breeds, this only benefits the dog's health and character.

EURASIAN

Height	19–24 in (48–60 cm)
Weight	40–70 lbs (18–32 kg)
Coat	profuse, medium long, hugging the body loosely, with thick undercoat
Color	any shade from red to wolf-gray, black, black and tan

Grooming

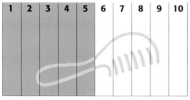

Required Exercise

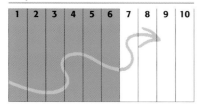

Suitability for City Living

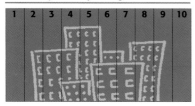

Common Health Problems

Suitable for first-time owners

The **EURASIAN** is a new German breed, the result of a single breeder's work. Julius Wipfel wanted to create a dog that would not only be an ideal family dog, but also look very beautiful. To achieve this he crossbred Chow Chows and members of the Spitz family and added some Samoyed blood to the mix. The dog that resulted, the Eurasian, loves children and is very affectionate, sensitive, and loving. Given these qualities, it is not surprising that this dog requires a lot of love and attention from its people. Obviously, it cannot simply be parked in the garden or yard. Instead it wants to be included in everything that is happening. It is self-confident and athletic, but doesn't require huge amounts of exercise. Its coat sheds dirt and is less thick than that of the dogs from which the breed originated. That is why it needs relatively little grooming in spite of its bear-like looks. The Eurasian is reserved with strangers and a good watchdog, but becomes very friendly and interested once it has been introduced to a newcomer.

Height	18 in (46 cm)
Weight	35.2–40 lbs (16–22.5 kg)
Coat	relatively long, dense, silky, glossy, heavily fringed
Color	uniform black, liver, golden brown, or mahogany red

The **FIELD SPANIEL** has the most pleasant personality of all the spaniels, and yet is one of the rarest breeds of this group. Because it is considerably heavier, and therefore less elegant than the Cocker or the Springer Spaniel, most people have never heard of it. Yet, it deserves greater appreciation as a tranquil, loyal, devoted, and intelligent family dog of great gentleness. It does, however, still have the genes of a hunting spaniel, and therefore needs a lot of walking and other exercise. It can also become quite destructive if it is left alone too much. The Field Spaniel is generally very suspicious of strangers and should be taught as a puppy to get used to new people, loud noises, and unfamiliar sounds.

Grooming

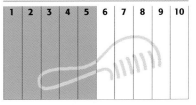

1	2	3	4	5	6	7	8	9	10

Required Exercise

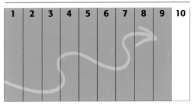

1	2	3	4	5	6	7	8	9	10

Suitability for City Living

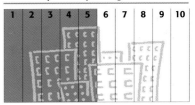

1	2	3	4	5	6	7	8	9	10

Common Health Problems

hip dysplasia, retinal atrophy

Suitable for first-time owners

FLAT-COATED RETRIEVER

Height	approximately 24 in (60 cm)
Weight	approximately 66–77 lbs (30–35 kg)
Coat	long, dense, fine, smooth
Color	black or liver

Grooming

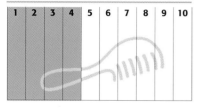

1	2	3	4	5	6	7	8	9	10

Required Exercise

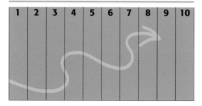

1	2	3	4	5	6	7	8	9	10

Suitability for City Living

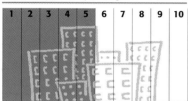

1	2	3	4	5	6	7	8	9	10

Common Health Problems

hip dysplasia

Suitable for first-time owners

The **FLAT-COATED RETRIEVER** was bred in England in the nineteenth century, probably from a combination of Newfoundlands and Labrador Retrievers. The Flat-coated Retriever is a solidly built, strong, and well-muscled hunting and retrieving dog with an excellent nose. At the same time, it is a great family dog. It is fantastic with children and pleasant, affectionate, and cheerful with the rest of the family. The Flat-coated Retriever can be kept in the city if it gets at least two and a half hours of exercise a day, including swimming, playing ball, and retrieving sticks. But it is quite useless as a watchdog because it finds all people irresistible. It adores its master and is, for this reason, easy to train. It wants to learn and to please and loves praise and rewards. Much more outgoing and friendly than most hunting breeds, the Flat-coated Retriever is more like the Golden and Labrador Retriever in its love for people. In fact, its only flaw may be the exuberance with which it welcomes visitors, and its tendency to jump up on everybody. But its beauty, robust nature, and loyal character more than make up for this minor shortcoming.

Height	15 in (39 cm)
Weight	approximately 16 lbs (8 kg)
Coat	smooth variety: straight, dense, short, waterproof, with soft undercoat; wire-haired variety: dense, hard, curly
Color	the base color is white and always dominant, with tan, black, or black and tan markings

The **FOX TERRIER** is one of the most energetic, impulsive, lively, and scrappy of terriers—or perhaps of all dogs. There are two varieties of this breed: the Wire-haired Terrier and the Smooth Terrier. Cynocologists regard them as two separate breeds, but in effect the dogs differ only in the quality of their coat. A Fox Terrier never seems to run out of steam. Its mission in life is to play, and no future Fox Terrier owner should underestimate how much time will be spent throwing balls during the next 10 or 12 years. The Fox Terrier loves its family and is devoted, vigilant, cheerful, and rugged. It is a good playmate for children, but does have a strong hunting instinct and should not be left alone with guinea pigs or other small pets. Fox Terriers can live wherever people live, but do need a lot of exercise so that their indomitable energy does not become unbearable for its people. These dogs have powerful jaws and strong teeth, and they love to tussle. Essentially, the Fox Terrier is anything but a lap dog, and it needs firm treatment and thorough training that has to be started early and kept up for a long time.

Grooming

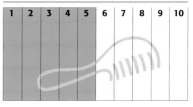

| 1 | 2 | 3 | 4 | 5 | 6 | 7 | 8 | 9 | 10 |

Required Exercise

| 1 | 2 | 3 | 4 | 5 | 6 | 7 | 8 | 9 | 10 |

Suitability for City Living

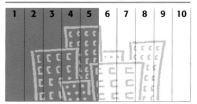

| 1 | 2 | 3 | 4 | 5 | 6 | 7 | 8 | 9 | 10 |

Common Health Problems

allergies, eczema

For experienced dog owners

FRENCH BULLDOG

Height	12 in (30 cm)
Weight	13–26 lbs (6–12 kg)
Coat	short, glossy, soft
Color	bringé (or tiger): black and not too dark reddish-yellow brindle; ground color white, with tiger markings

Grooming

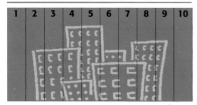

1	2	3	4	5	6	7	8	9	10

Required Exercise

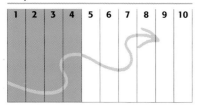

1	2	3	4	5	6	7	8	9	10

Suitability for City Living

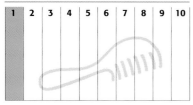

1	2	3	4	5	6	7	8	9	10

The **FRENCH BULLDOG** has been appreciated as a wonderful companion dog since the end of the last century. The English claim that the French Bulldog is a miniature version of the much heavier English Bulldog that the English did not like and exported to France. The French, for their part, claim the breed is purely French. No matter what its nationality, if there is such a thing as a perfect apartment dog, the French Bulldog is it. It is a clean, pleasant dog that practically does not shed, is easy to train, has no bad habits, and requires very little exercise. The ideal home for a French Bulldog is a household of older people with neither children nor other pets whom the dog might consider rivals for affection. The French Bulldog is happiest if it is the focus of all attention and love. This does not mean that this breed should not be around children. French Bulldogs often live contentedly in average families and are generally quite good at adapting to most situations. They don't make much work, but they are not happy unless they can be close to their favorite person.

Common Health Problems

respiratory problems, eye injuries

Suitable for first-time owners

Height	24–27 in (60–68 cm)
Weight	110–143 lbs (50–65 kg)
Coat	fine, short, soft
Color	all shades of mahogany

Grooming

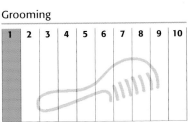

1	2	3	4	5	6	7	8	9	10

Required Exercise

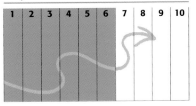

1	2	3	4	5	6	7	8	9	10

Suitability for City Living

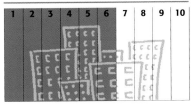

1	2	3	4	5	6	7	8	9	10

The **FRENCH MASTIFF** is thought to be one of the world's oldest breeds. The most striking feature of this dog is the heavy, expressive head. The ancestors of this breed were probably the Bulldog and the Bullmastiff. This was the dog that accompanied knights, warriors, and conquerors on their forays. It was also used for hunting jaguars and bears, as a guard dog, and for herding cattle. Today no one needs to be a warrior or conqueror to keep this dog. In spite of its powerful jaws and fear-inspiring appearance, the modern French Mastiff is a good-natured, friendly family dog that gets along famously with children and loves to be loved. The French Mastiff is suspicious of strangers and therefore a good watchdog in spite of its quiet, loving nature. Toward other dogs it can be aggressive, however, and that is why obedience training administered with kindness and firmness is an absolute must. Once this strong and heavy dog has made up its mind to go in a certain direction, it is very difficult both physically and psychologically to stop it. In spite of its bulk the French Mastiff is amazingly athletic and fast, and it needs regular walks and other exercise to develop a harmonious balance of body muscle.

Common Health Problems

hip dysplasia, ectropion

Suitable for first-time owners

GERMAN HOUND

Height	16–21 in (40–53 cm)
Weight	approximately 35 lbs (16 kg)
Coat	sleek, lying close to the body, short
Color	white with other colors, red and other colors, tan; usually with white markings

Grooming

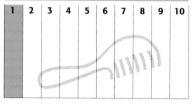

Required Exercise

Suitability for City Living

Common Health Problems

For experienced dog owners

The **GERMAN HOUND** is an outstanding hunting dog, fast, eager to work, tenacious, tough, indifferent to bad weather, and has a loud, clear voice. At the beginning of this century, a number of different hound breeds were combined to create a versatile "hound of all work." The German Hound has a very fine nose and is used for all methods of hunting fox, rabbit, and wild boar. This dog should be kept only by active hunters; the leisure of a non-working life is anathema to it.

Height	up to 16 in (40 cm)
Weight	20–22 lbs (9–10 kg)
Coat	smooth or wire-haired; short and hard in either case
Color	black, black mixed with gray, or dark brown; all with tan markings

The **GERMAN HUNTING TERRIER** is only for hunters. It is a true one-man dog and has an incredible passion for hunting. It lacks all talent as a companion dog; instead it has all the working qualities a hunter could wish for, pursuing prey both underground in dens and lairs, and above ground. But it has no social skills whatsoever. The German Hunting Terrier is courageous to a fault, aggressive, and pig-headed. There is nothing it is afraid of, and it doesn't hesitate to attack even wild boars, which can be truly dangerous. It also goes after deer, foxes, badgers, and even birds. If asked to guard the house or car, it takes this job very seriously, too.

Grooming

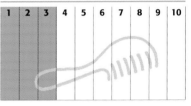

1	2	3	4	5	6	7	8	9	10

Required Exercise

1	2	3	4	5	6	7	8	9	10

Suitability for City Living

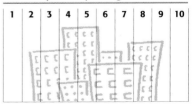

1	2	3	4	5	6	7	8	9	10

Common Health Problems

For experienced dog owners

GERMAN LONG-HAIRED POINTER

Height	male: 25–26 in (63–66 cm); female: 24–25 in (60–63 cm)
Weight	approximately 48–70 lbs (22–32 kg)
Coat	hair about 1 in long, flat, lying close to the body; hard, with a thick undercoat
Color	brown with or without white markings, brown roan, light roan, trout tiger

Grooming

1	2	3	4	5	6	7	8	9	10

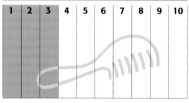

Required Exercise

1	2	3	4	5	6	7	8	9	10

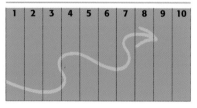

Suitability for City Living

1	2	3	4	5	6	7	8	9	10

Common Health Problems

rare hip dysplasia

For experienced dog owners

The **GERMAN LONG-HAIRED POINTER** is an excellent all-around hunting dog with a special talent for working in the woods and in water, and if the German Long-haired Dog Club has anything to say about it, it will remain exclusively a hunting dog. It is definitely a separate breed, not a variant of the German Wire-haired or the German Short-haired Pointer. This dog is practically unknown outside of Germany, but deserves wider appreciation as an extremely versatile dog of great speed and endurance; it is also indifferent to the cold and has a very fine nose. It is totally unsuited for living in the city, having been bred to work as a hunting dog. It can display its outstanding qualities only in the field. The German Longhair is calm and steady and especially good at intensive searches. It is a very friendly dog because the standard of the German Long-haired Club forbids any trace of aggressiveness toward humans and other dogs. The German Long-haired Pointer is expected to behave normally in a pack, and if a dog doesn't, it is disqualified for having a "character flaw."

Height	22–26 in (55–65 cm)
Weight	62–77 lbs (28–35 kg)
Coat	weatherproof, dense; with regular-length or longer guard hair
Color	black or gray either uniform or with light or brown markings; black with regular brown, yellow to light gray markings

The **GERMAN SHEPHERD** is one of the world's most popular dogs. Savior of people in distress, rescuing them from fires and avalanches, helper of the disabled, police dog, war dog, narcotics detective, herding dog, star in films and on television—listing all its roles and accomplishments would fill pages. The crucial character element of this breed is its adaptability. Ideally this dog is reliable, self-confident, bold, obedient, loyal, and even-tempered. It should never be nervous or timid. Any breeder who offers even one shy or nervous dog for sale should be avoided, because a nervous German Shepherd is a potentially dangerous dog. A well-adjusted German Shepherd, on the other hand, can be taught just about anything. Unfortunately, many owners are interested primarily in training it as a guard dog. The German Shepherd is by nature vigilant and protects its family effectively; it needs no further training in this line. As a well-brought-up family dog, it has all the qualities one could wish for: It is intelligent and alert, approaches strangers cautiously, but never with malice, is loyal and devoted to its family and tolerant toward other animals. It is basically a working dog, and it is not happy unless it has plenty of physical activity, daily obedience exercises, and tasks to perform. The German Shepherd needs a master who is as intelligent and capable as it is; this dog is wasted on anyone else.

Grooming

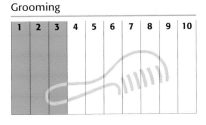

| 1 | 2 | 3 | 4 | 5 | 6 | 7 | 8 | 9 | 10 |

Required Exercise

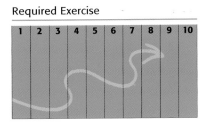

| 1 | 2 | 3 | 4 | 5 | 6 | 7 | 8 | 9 | 10 |

Suitability for City Living

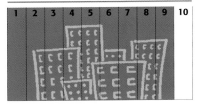

| 1 | 2 | 3 | 4 | 5 | 6 | 7 | 8 | 9 | 10 |

Common Health Problems

hip dysplasia, panostitis, epilepsy, allergies, pannus

For experienced dog owners

GERMAN SHORT-HAIRED POINTER

Height	male: 23–26 in (58–65 cm); female: 21–23 in (53–59 cm)
Weight	approximately 48–70 lbs (22–32 kg)
Coat	short, flat, somewhat coarse
Color	brown, brown with white or roan markings or patches, light or dark roan with or without white patches

Grooming

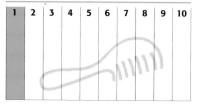

Required Exercise

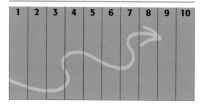

Suitability for City Living

Common Health Problems

rare hip dysplasia

For experienced dog owners

The **GERMAN SHORT-HAIRED POINTER** was bred in the seventeenth century, probably by crossing Spanish pointers with bloodhounds, with the intent of creating an all-purpose hunting dog. It is a tracking hound, pointer, and retriever all in one, adapts to any climate, and is highly trainable. At the same time, it is probably the best family dog among all the hunting breeds, with its idea of happiness being to lie on the sofa in the evening cuddled up next to its people. The German Shorthair is attentive, frank, resolute, cheerful, and easy to teach, quickly grasping and mastering whatever it is asked to learn. It loves children and makes a wonderful playmate, as well as a perfect companion and friend. It is never moody or malicious. But it cannot be kept in an apartment or in the city. This dog is filled with high-spirited enthusiasm and energy, and needs lots of physical activity. After all, the beauty of this dog lies in the way it moves. The ease with which it covers the ground in big bounds is what is so characteristic of the German Shorthair. If kept in the city, it may become hyperactive and out of control, losing its dignity and the benefits of its intelligence. You don't necessarily have to be a hunter to keep a German Shorthair, but you do have to enjoy long walks, doing subordination exercises with the dog, and presenting it with challenges. No one should expect the wonderful innate qualities of this dog to survive under the confining conditions of the city with its asphalt streets.

Height	18–22 in (45–54 cm)
Weight	approximately 44 lbs (20 kg)
Coat	thick and wavy, glossy, lying close to the body
Color	brown and brown roan

The **GERMAN SPANIEL** is a sporting breed created for working in forest, field, and water. It has a superb nose, and is a passionate and aggressive hunter that lays hold of the game with a sure and deadly grip. This dog is extremely courageous, hardy, and tough. It obeys and follows its master, but it is so exclusively devoted to hunting that interaction with humans is secondary, and not very important to it. It, therefore, does not make a good companion dog. The German Spaniel wants to work, and that is the way it should stay.

Grooming

1	2	3	4	5	6	7	8	9	10

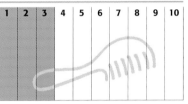

Required Exercise

1	2	3	4	5	6	7	8	9	10

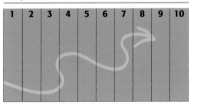

Suitability for City Living

1	2	3	4	5	6	7	8	9	10

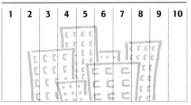

Common Health Problems

For experienced dog owners

GERMAN SPITZ

Height	Wolfsspitz: 20 in (50 cm); Grossspitz: 18 in (46 cm); Mittelspitz: 13 in (34 cm); Kleinspitz: 10 in (26 cm); Zwergspitz: 8 in (20 cm)
Weight	Wolfsspitz: male, 48 lbs (22 kg); female, 40 lbs (18 kg); Mittelspitz: 18–22 lbs (8–10 kg); Kleinspitz: 11–13 lbs (5–6 kg); Zwergspitz: 6 lbs (2.5 kg)
Coat	thick all over the body, short on muzzle, ears, and paws
Color	Wolfsspitz: silver-gray with black shading; Grossspitz: white, brown, or black; Mittelspitz and Kleinspitz: white, brown, black, orange, gray-ticked

Grooming

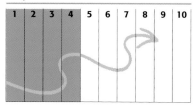

Required Exercise

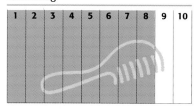

Suitability for City Living

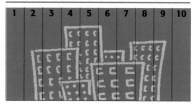

Common Health Problems

Suitable for first-time owners

The members of the **GERMAN SPITZ** family are very ancient dogs. They were already popular in the Stone Age. Later they were typically kept by farmers, and finally, in the 1950s, they became the dog everyone wanted to own. Then some exotic breed replaced it, and the Spitz acquired the unjustified reputation of being a constant barker, and disappeared almost completely from the scene.

This is a great pity because the Spitz, in any of its sizes, is the perfect companion dog. It is as uncomplicated as a dog can be, lively, absolutely adaptable, and very focused on its humans. It has not a trace of hunting instinct and gets along with all other animals. If it grows up with children, it makes an unsurpassed baby-sitter, putting up with being dressed and having things like crayons stuck up its nose. And it has a fabulous sense of humor to boot. The Spitz is an excellent watchdog who approaches strangers with suspicion, but not aggressively. Its tendency to bark a lot can be kept within bounds if the dog is taught early to resist the impulse. The Spitz is extremely intelligent and easy to train; it also learns tricks easily—after all, the smallest members of the family, the Zwergspitz, are popular circus dogs. The Spitz thrives in the spring, fall, and winter, but suffers in the hot summer weather because of its thick, heavy coat. This magnificent coat has to be brushed regularly; apart from that, it is practically self-cleaning.

Height	male: 24–26 in (60–67 cm); female: 22–24 in (55–60 cm)
Weight	62–77 lbs (28–35 kg)
Coat	hard, weather-resistant wire hair, double-coated
Color	brown, brown or black roan (i.e., with a heavy sprinkling of white hairs)

The **GERMAN WIRE-HAIRED POINTER** is everything a hunter could wish for: an infallible retriever, a pointer, and a steady, reliable, and hard-working friend and hunting companion. Its coat, which requires practically no care, offers protection against all kinds of weather and against the underbrush of even the roughest terrain. The wiry hair sheds dirt like water. The German Wire-haired Pointer has a natural inclination to be a watchdog, and is generally suspicious of strangers, but not aggressive toward them. But this dog does not belong in the city. It is bred for field work and can develop its special qualities only under these conditions. Given a setting that accommodates its particular needs, the German Wire-haired is beyond compare. It can be kept as a family dog if the family lives in the country, and if it is given enough work and exercise. It has a great need for human companionship and is friendly, affectionate, and even-tempered. German Wire-haireds definitely can be willful and need owners who don't overestimate themselves, or underestimate their dogs.

Grooming

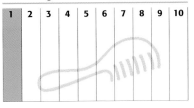

1	2	3	4	5	6	7	8	9	10

Required Exercise

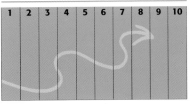

1	2	3	4	5	6	7	8	9	10

Suitability for City Living

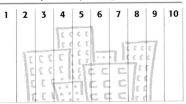

1	2	3	4	5	6	7	8	9	10

Common Health Problems

entropion, hip dysplasia

For experienced dog owners

GIANT SCHNAUZER

Height	26–28 in (65–70 cm)
Weight	approximately 77 lbs (35 kg)
Coat	wiry, hard, with a soft undercoat
Color	black, salt and pepper

Grooming

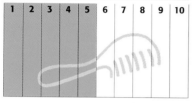

1	2	3	4	5	6	7	8	9	10

Required Exercise

1	2	3	4	5	6	7	8	9	10

Suitability for City Living

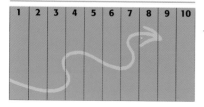

1	2	3	4	5	6	7	8	9	10

Common Health Problems

hip dysplasia

Suitable for first-time owners

The **GIANT SCHNAUZER** is a larger version of the Standard Schnauzer and, like all Schnauzers, it owes its name to its elegant beard. ("Schnauz" is German for "whiskers.") The Giant Schnauzer is a little quieter than the Standard, but also somewhat bolder and more aggressive, with a highly developed protective instinct. Schnauzers in general have a rather intimidating appearance, which in this case is increased by the breed's size. The Giant Schnauzer makes an excellent police and guard dog, but it also adapts beautifully to its family. As long as it is allowed to be part of everything, it is happy. Since it is quiet and very tolerant with children, it makes an ideal family dog, squarely built, practical, and well behaved. It has to be stripped twice a year, but requires no special grooming otherwise. It is a very active dog that loves its people and everything they do, is attentive, rugged, and tough, and carefully looks over all newcomers. Like its smaller cousins, the Giant Schnauzer is very intelligent, willing to work, and eager to learn, but can turn aggressive if treated too harshly. Training has to start early and be intensive and consistent. The Giant Schnauzer rebels against unfair treatment but is able, under appropriately friendly and authoritative guidance, to master everything a dog needs to know to become a happy household companion and be appreciated by its human family members.

Height	male: 14 in (35.5 cm); female: 13 in (33 cm)
Weight	29–35 lbs (13–16 kg)
Coat	guard hair is hard; undercoat and hair on head are soft
Color	wheat, blue, brindle

The **GLEN OF IMAAL TERRIER** is a dog with a double personality. This is apparent even in its very appearance. It is a large dog on short legs, and an affectionate, cuddly pet for children, but has teeth as strong as a German Shepherd's. A true terrier, the Glen of Imaal is rather aggressive toward other dogs and a ferocious hunter of vermin. However, appropriate training can counteract these aggressive impulses. The Glen of Imaal is vigilant like all terriers and has good guarding instincts, but is not an excessive barker. Actually, its voice is very pleasant sounding and quite low. The Imaal is totally devoted to its family, but will try again and again as long as it lives to test limits. That is why fair and consistent training is important from the very beginning. The Glen of Imaal may look like an utterly innocent and charming bundle of fluff, but don't forget that inside is a tough and stoic working dog bred to hunt fox and badgers. Yet, in its heart of hearts it loves peace.

Grooming

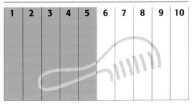

1	2	3	4	5	6	7	8	9	10

Required Exercise

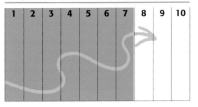

1	2	3	4	5	6	7	8	9	10

Suitability for City Living

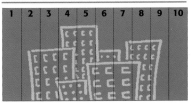

1	2	3	4	5	6	7	8	9	10

Common Health Problems

Suitable for first-time owners

GOLDEN RETRIEVER

Height	male: 22–24 in (56–61 cm); female: 20–22 in (51–56 cm)
Weight	male: 70–81 lbs (32–37 kg); female: 59–70 lbs (27–32 kg)
Coat	straight or slightly wavy guard hair with feathering, waterproof undercoat
Color	all shades of gold and wheat; any hint of red is a defect

Grooming

1	2	3	4	5	6	7	8	9	10

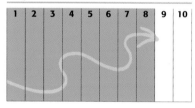

Required Exercise

1	2	3	4	5	6	7	8	9	10

Suitability for City Living

1	2	3	4	5	6	7	8	9	10

Common Health Problems

hip dysplasia, cartilage defects during growth, hypothyroidism, progressive deterioration of the retina

Suitable for first-time owners

The **GOLDEN RETRIEVER** is really a wonderful dog. An excellent hunting dog endowed with great intelligence and a fine nose, the Golden Retriever is unaffected by bad weather and—like all retrievers—a passionate swimmer; it is also an obedient pet, responsive to training, affable, patient with children, and happy to live together with whatever other pets exist in the household. This is not a one-man dog, but a dog for the entire family. It likes all humans, and is therefore no good as a guard dog.

Its beauty and its pleasant, gentle nature have made the Golden Retriever very popular as a companion dog, and that has become something of a problem. Although the Golden can adapt to living in the city (it adapts to any situation as long as it can be with its people), it is really an outdoor dog that needs a lot of exercise—at least two hours a day in any weather. If given tasks to perform, the Golden Retriever develops quite amazing abilities, which is why it is such a good seeing-eye dog and narcotics detective.

Unfortunately, the huge popularity of the Golden Retriever has led many dealers and breeders of doubtful ethics to become interested in this breed, with the result that nowadays one not infrequently runs into defective and rather stupid representatives of the breed. There are even Golden Retrievers that fight with other dogs and bite, which used to be unheard of. It is important to seek out a reputable breeder if you want to buy a Golden Retriever.

Height	male: 26 in (66 cm); female: 24 in (62 cm)
Weight	male: 55–79 lbs (25–36 kg); female: 44–68 lbs (20–31 kg)
Coat	long, silky
Color	black and tan

The breed of the **GORDON SETTER** was developed in Scotland by the fourth Duke of Gordon toward the end of the eighteenth century. It is hard to understand why the Irish and the English Setter are so much more popular than the Gordon. They may be somewhat faster and more agile in the hunt, but that is the only edge they have over the Gordon, which is a near-perfect companion both in the field and in everyday life. It can, if necessary, be kept in the city, but remember that this is a fairly large hunting dog that was bred to run and needs plenty of room to display the flowing, powerful gait with head raised high that is typical of the breed. The Gordon is generally calmer and more stable than the Irish Setter, as long as it gets enough exercise and work to do. "Work to do," in the case of hunting dogs, means obedience and retrieving exercises. Walks alone are not enough. Although an active dog, the Gordon Setter is even-tempered, humorous, a good watchdog, and a wonderful family dog. It can be rather obstinate but is, like all setters, extremely sensitive. Early and patient subordination training is important. The Gordon needs to be with people, but its fondness for humans is concentrated on the intimate circle of its immediate world and does not necessarily extend to unfamiliar visitors.

Grooming

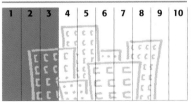

Required Exercise

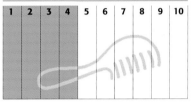

Suitability for City Living

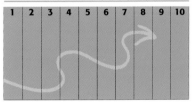

Common Health Problems

occasionally hip dysplasia, progressive retinal atrophy, rare epilepsy

Suitable for first-time owners

GREAT DANE

Height	male: 31 in (at least 80 cm); female: at least 28 in (72 cm)
Weight	approximately 110 lbs (50 kg)
Coat	very short, dense, glossy
Color	black, blue, fawn, brindle, harlequin (white with black patches)

Grooming

1	2	3	4	5	6	7	8	9	10

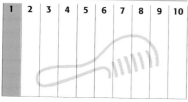

Required Exercise

1	2	3	4	5	6	7	8	9	10

Suitability for City Living

1	2	3	4	5	6	7	8	9	10

Common Health Problems

hip dysplasia, cancer of the bone, heart disease, tumors, joint dislocations

For experienced dog owners

The **GREAT DANE**, or **GERMAN MASTIFF**, can be traced back to about the fourteenth century in Central Europe, where it was originally developed to hunt wild boar. In those days, the nobility considered it entertainment to ride out after boar with a whole pack of thoroughbred dogs. These dogs had to be fast, strong, untiring, and reliable. Because the Great Dane was such a magnificent-looking animal, the aristocrats also liked to show them off next to the fireplace in their great castles. As its history implies, the Great Dane needs a lot of running and exercise. At the same time, it is gentle, well mannered, normally quiet, and affectionate toward its master and family. It is also a hit with children if it has learned early on to behave cautiously around them. It is never mean or malicious toward strangers, although it can of course function as an impressive watchdog. It must be stressed, though, that a dog of this size should never be trained to attack or behave aggressively. Some people actually keep Great Danes in apartments, but this is not a good idea unless you can let your dog run at least 9 miles a day so that it won't get stiff and develop weak bones and muscles. Unfortunately, Great Danes don't grow very old. The most to be expected is 9 or 10 happy years with their family. The Great Dane is one of the handsomest breeds, but it is very big, and thus needs plenty of space and impressive amounts of food. It also requires first-class obedience training, for which it is often a good idea to get professional help.

Height	male: 27–32 in (68.5–81 cm); female: 25–29 in (63.5–74 cm)
Weight	88–123 lbs (40–56 kg)
Coat	double coat of very thick, long or medium-long hair that is somewhat longer on the neck, tail, and hind legs
Color	pure white; gray, tan, or badger-colored markings permitted

Grooming

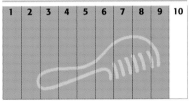

Required Exercise

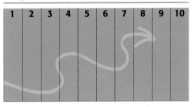

Suitability for City Living

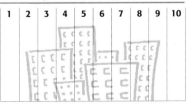

Common Health Problems

hip dysplasia, eyelid abnormalities, epilepsy

For experienced dog owners

The **GREAT PYRENEES** has a long and honorable past as a watchdog and herding dog, whose task it was to fight off wolves and bears. It is a huge dog with unusually varied qualities. It will defend its family to the point of death and attack anything and anyone that threatens them. At the same time, it is very loving and sensitive to human moods, incredibly patient with children, and an excellent babysitter. It is quiet, serious, and very conscientious, but does need a great deal of space and physical activity, so it really should live only on an extensive property in the country. It loves the cold and usually prefers not to be indoors. It is friendly and affable toward strangers, and normally does not get into fights. However, some Great Pyrenees tend to be one-man dogs, and it is important to socialize one's dog early and well.

The Great Pyrenees is indisputably a very handsome dog, and irresistible as a puppy. But anyone contemplating buying a puppy has to realize that this dog needs lots of exercise, and that at least one member of the family has to enjoy taking very long walks. This dog is very independent and trusts its own judgment best (especially the males); obedience training is therefore crucial, and takes a lot of time, persistence, and patience.

GREATER SWISS MOUNTAIN DOG

Height	male: 26–28 in (65–72 cm)
	female: 23–27 in (58–68 cm)
Weight	approximately 88 lbs (40 kg)
Coat	short, thick, glossy
Color	ebony black, with white on paws, face, chest, and tip of tail; always with tan markings

Grooming

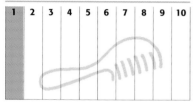

Required Exercise

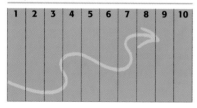

Suitability for City Living

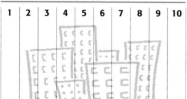

Common Health Problems

hip dysplasia

For experienced dog owners

The **GREATER SWISS MOUNTAIN DOG** is said to be a direct descendent of Julius Caesar's Molossian dogs. It was originally kept by butchers as a watch- and guard dog, as well as a draft animal that pulled heavy carts to the market. It also protected the cattle. The Greater Swiss Mountain Dog is very vigilant and suspicious of strangers, but it is a great family dog: even-tempered, quiet, patient, intelligent, and reliable. Although it behaves well indoors, it needs a lot of space and movement, preferably on the owner's property, which it will happily guard. But the Greater Swiss is not made for city life. It is not a dog to keep in the yard because it needs the presence of, and interaction with, its people. It gets along well with other animals and is responsive to training.

Height	male: 28–31 in (71–78 cm); female: 27–28 in (68.5–71 cm)
Weight	55–66 lbs (25–30 kg)
Coat	short, smooth, lying flat to the body
Color	all colors, with or without white markings

The **GREYHOUND** can reach speeds up to 43 miles per hour. It has been bred for thousands of years to hunt other animals, but today it is used mostly to chase mechanical rabbits on racetracks. The cruelties associated with the racing "industry" are too horrible to be discussed here. This is indeed a sad fate for a truly outstanding breed of dogs. Greyhounds make wonderful pets because they are quiet, friendly, restrained, very clean, and have a coat that requires no care whatsoever. They are often referred to as "40 mph couch potatoes" and require between 10 and 30 minutes of exercise a day. The Greyhound has a fantastic sense of humor, and it is a pleasure to have around. Training these dogs is very easy, if done the right way. Never uncooperative or obstinate, the Greyhound is extremely sensitive, somewhat nervous, and easily distracted. Gentle and patient obedience training can do wonders to enhance the self-confidence of this delightful dog. The Greyhound belongs in the home of a family that lives quietly, but whose members are athletic. Remember that this dog was bred for running long before the first pyramids were built; this is a heritage that must not be ignored.

Grooming

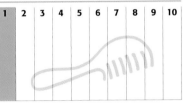

1	2	3	4	5	6	7	8	9	10

Required Exercise

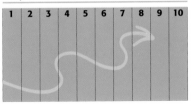

1	2	3	4	5	6	7	8	9	10

Suitability for City Living

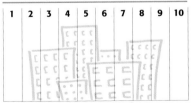

1	2	3	4	5	6	7	8	9	10

Common Health Problems

For experienced dog owners

GROSSER MÜNSTERLÄNDER

Height	male: approximately 24 in (61 cm); female: approximately 23 in (59 cm)
Weight	55–64 lbs (25–29 kg)
Coat	long and dense, straight; hair on head, short and flat
Color	white with black patches or dots, or black-speckled

Grooming

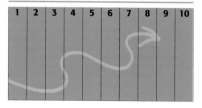

Required Exercise

Suitability for City Living

The **GROSSER MÜNSTERLÄNDER** is one of the oldest German sporting breeds and probably was first developed to kill hawks. It is an ideal all-purpose bird dog that both points and retrieves. It can be used in any terrain, never tires, and is unaffected by bad weather. Hunters especially appreciate its sharp intelligence, sureness in following a scent, and precision of retrieving. It can be trained easily, is a fierce enemy of predators, and can also be kept as a watchdog. The Grosser Münsterländer is a cheerful, very active dog that craves work and is not well suited for the idle life of a city dog. It has the qualities that make for a wonderful family dog, namely, immense loyalty, affection, and trustworthiness. It needs a great deal of exercise along with things to keep it occupied and should, if at all possible, have a chance to swim.

Common Health Problems

rare hip dysplasia

Suitable for first-time owners

Height	22–24 in (56–60 cm)
Weight	84–99 lbs (38–45 kg)
Coat	short, dense, thick, smooth, elastic
Color	light to dark cherry-red, more or less brindled, with or without a mask; small white spots on chest permitted

The **HANOVER HOUND** is a very rare breed that derives from hound varieties that are two thousand years old. Around the year 1800, the Electorate of Hanover became a kind of refuge for the breed when, in consequence of the general decline of hunting, it was threatened with extinction. Today, the Hanover Hound is kept on a leash during hunts and is used exclusively for tracking wounded ungulates. It is not a companion dog.

Grooming

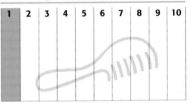

1	2	3	4	5	6	7	8	9	10

Required Exercise

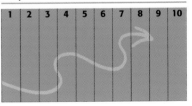

1	2	3	4	5	6	7	8	9	10

Suitability for City Living

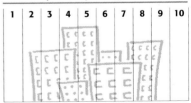

1	2	3	4	5	6	7	8	9	10

Common Health Problems

For experienced dog owners

HAVANESE

Height	8–11 in (20–28 cm)
Weight	13 lbs (6 kg)
Coat	long, silky, somewhat wavy
Color	all shades of brown, also gold, white, champagne, and gray; with or without white areas

Grooming

Required Exercise

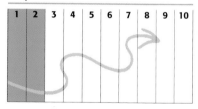

Suitability for City Living

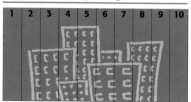

The **HAVANESE** is a delight. Lively and always in good spirits, it will often master the most amazing tricks all by itself, just to get everyone's attention. Its greatest desire is to be included in whatever is happening. Perhaps this trait has something to do with the breed's romantic history. The Havanese was a great favorite of the wealthy upper class of Cuba, and when these people had to leave the country during the Cuban Revolution, some of them took their dogs along as they fled. The Havanese is still quite rare, but it is an adorable little companion dog, and could become a fabulous circus dog and trick performer. It is very intelligent and responds well to obedience training, which is needed because with its great charm, the Havanese will try to run the entire household. The silky coat has to be brushed every other day, but that is just about all the grooming that is required.

Common Health Problems

Suitable for first-time owners

Height	male: 24–28 in (60–70 cm); female: 22–26 in (55–65 cm)
Weight	male: 66–88 lbs (30–40 kg); female: 55–77 lbs (25–35 kg)
Coat	slightly wavy, rather coarse long hair
Color	black, blond, black with tan areas

Grooming

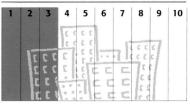

1	2	3	4	5	6	7	8	9	10

Required Exercise

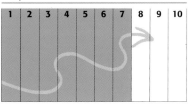

1	2	3	4	5	6	7	8	9	10

Suitability for City Living

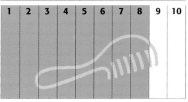

1	2	3	4	5	6	7	8	9	10

The **HOVAWART**'s name derives from the German word "Hofwart," which means caretaker of the farmstead, and during the Middle Ages the Hovawart served as watchdog on large German farms. This job required a dog that was smart, reliable, loyal, could tell good people from the bad, and never ran off. The modern Hovawart still lives up to this tradition. It adapts very well to its family and will be content either to accompany its people on walks or to take part in more ambitious sports. But it does need firm and consistent subordination training. Though devoted to its master, it is very stubborn and headstrong. A female is preferable as a first dog because females are less determined than males to test their position within the family hierarchy. Also, because of its size and weight, the Hovawart is not an appropriate dog for people with a weak constitution. It is slow to grow up and acts like an overgrown baby for at least two years. It has to be well socialized from the beginning—like all dogs—and exposed to different situations so that it will develop into an adult dog of stoic calm with nerves of steel. The Hovawart has to be allowed to be close to its people; it loves children and has a natural protective instinct. This dog should not be trained as a guard dog; its size alone is enough to impress any intruder, and an aggressive Hovawart can be really dangerous.

Common Health Problems

rare hip dysplasia, shortened lower jaw

Suitable for first-time owners

IRISH SETTER

Height	25–27 in (63–68 cm)
Weight	59–68 lbs (27–31 kg)
Coat	long, silky
Color	mahogany

Grooming

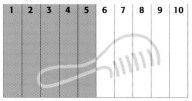

1	2	3	4	5	6	7	8	9	10

Required Exercise

1	2	3	4	5	6	7	8	9	10

Suitability for City Living

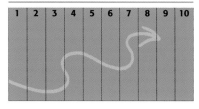

1	2	3	4	5	6	7	8	9	10

Common Health Problems

rare hip dysplasia, epilepsy, twisted stomach

Suitable for first-time owners

The **IRISH SETTER** is one of the most beautiful pointers and probably the best known of the setters. However, its lovely looks have had some tragic consequences. The rich red color of its coat has gained it great popularity, and as a result the Irish Setter has been reduced to playing the role of companion dog. This is a complete waste of this breed's excellent nose and love of retrieving. Mass breeders and dealers started producing Irish Setters, many of whom soon became unreliable, hyperactive, and nervous. However, the fad has passed, and the breed has been able to recover to a large extent. Still, if you are interested in an Irish Setter, you should get it from a breeder who raises and trains the dogs to work as pointers.

A true Irish Setter is an enchanting dog, a clown, charming, even-tempered, intelligent, and free of aggressiveness. It depends entirely on human company and has to be trained early on with consistency and gentleness. With a dog as active and intelligent as the Irish Setter, lack of obedience can have disastrous consequences. Although very adaptable, the Irish Setter can be recommended for the city only with serious qualifications. This dog has to pretend to be able to run and work. An owner uninterested in hunting has to be a hunter and challenge the dog constantly with retrieving and subordination exercises. There is no sadder sight than a setter hopping around the elevator nervously hoping for the kind of exercise it needs, but lacks. On the other hand, an Irish Setter living with the right kind of owner has a charm and breathtaking beauty that is unsurpassed by any other breed.

Height	18–19 in (46–48 cm)
Weight	approximately 5 lbs (12.5 kg)
Coat	hard and wiry, with a soft undercoat
Color	red, wheat red, or yellowish-red

Grooming

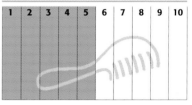

| 1 | 2 | 3 | 4 | 5 | 6 | 7 | 8 | 9 | 10 |

Required Exercise

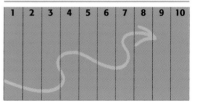

| 1 | 2 | 3 | 4 | 5 | 6 | 7 | 8 | 9 | 10 |

Suitability for City Living

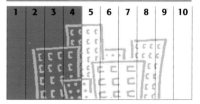

| 1 | 2 | 3 | 4 | 5 | 6 | 7 | 8 | 9 | 10 |

Common Health Problems

For experienced dog owners

The **IRISH TERRIER** is a true daredevil. Afraid of nothing and no one, it is impetuous, playful, and bold, attacking its opponent head on, fighting without thought of anything else, and never giving up. At the same time, it is a perfect gentleman. It is fast and untiring, loves its people with an immutable loyalty, and, with its infallible nose, will follow their scent over huge distances. It is everything a terrier is supposed to be, and anyone thinking of getting an Irish Terrier as a companion dog should bear this in mind. Affectionate and gentle with its master, it is capable of terrible ferociousness toward vermin—as well as toward other dogs it happens to dislike—displaying the reckless courage it is famous for. There is probably no other breed that is as tireless and adaptable as the Irish Terrier, as long as its master remains in charge. It needs strict discipline, but force will accomplish nothing with an Irish Terrier, or any other terrier for that matter. The Irish Terrier has a strong hunting instinct and is death to small predators. Of course, its idea of predator may not be the same as your neighbor's. When dealing with this breed, it is important that "No!" really mean "NO," and the dog may have to be reminded of this fact repeatedly.

IRISH WATER SPANIEL

Height	20–23 in (51–58 cm)
Weight	45–65 lbs (20.4–29.5 kg)
Coat	dense, tight curls all over the body, neck, and up to 4 in of the tail; not wooly; hair lubricated with natural skin secretion; hair on face and rest of tail is short
Color	liver

Grooming

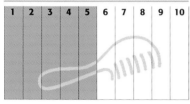

Required Exercise

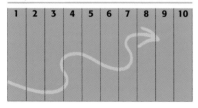

Suitability for City Living

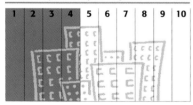

Common Health Problems

hip dysplasia, thyroid problems

For experienced dog owners

The **IRISH WATER SPANIEL** is quite different from all the other spaniels. It is a water dog, as is evident from its curly coat, from which the water drains as quickly as off a Poodle. The Irish Water Spaniel is a superb retriever of all kinds of game, persistent, courageous, reliable, and able to stay in icy water for hours at a time because of its very dense coat. It is obedient if given early and consistent training. Though it has an independent mind and is stubborn, it can learn just about anything if its master is patient and persistent enough. It is not the most ideal house dog because it can be aggressive toward strangers. For this reason, it is a better watchdog than most hunting breeds. But its natural distrust of people has to be guided since it is quite indiscriminate. But if this dog is well socialized early on, and given enough exercise and entertainment, it is a lot of fun. However, this is not a dog for very casual people who don't have the knack of asserting authority over their dog. But true dog lovers who can appreciate the breed's ability to work, its honesty, and its independence will be smitten with the Irish Water Spaniel.

IRISH WOLFHOUND

Height	24-34 in (62–86 cm)
Weight	male: at least 119 lbs (54 kg); female: at least 89 lbs (40.5 kg)
Coat	hard, rough, weather-resistant
Color	red, black, dun, white, fawn, wheaten, steel gray, brindle

The **IRISH WOLFHOUND** is the biggest and one of the strongest of all dogs. It has been called a "gentle giant," and that quality explains why it makes a wonderful family dog. It is reliable, patient, magnanimous, and intelligent. It adores its family and has a good instinct for recognizing danger. It is courageous, but never aggressive. Instead of biting, it prefers to knock down an intruder and stand over him or her, which never fails to impress the person so treated. The Irish Wolfhound cannot be kept in the city. The largest and heaviest of all the greyhounds, the Irish Wolfhound needs a lot of space and exercise. A farm or country estate is the ideal home for it. It has to be trained with firmness, but patiently and with empathy. It is much too large for disobedience to be tolerated. Training based on threat or use of force is inappropriate, and can turn this dog into a difficult and dangerously aggressive animal. Because these dogs grow so large so fast, you must make sure they get enough vitamins and minerals for proper development of the bones and muscles. The Irish Wolfhound is a very special dog and should be kept only by people who have the means to offer the world's largest dog the conditions it needs.

Grooming

1	2	3	4	5	6	7	8	9	10

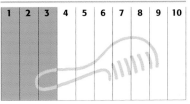

Required Exercise

1	2	3	4	5	6	7	8	9	10

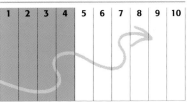

Suitability for City Living

1	2	3	4	5	6	7	8	9	10

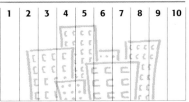

Common Health Problems

heart problems, hip dysplasia, lives only about 8 years

For experienced dog owners

ITALIAN GREYHOUND

Height	13–15 in (32–38 cm)
Weight	11 lbs (5 kg)
Coat	very short, fine
Color	fawn, blue, black, red, brown; often with white patches or markings

Grooming

Required Exercise

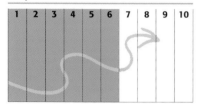

Suitability for City Living

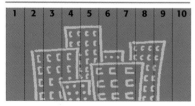

Common Health Problems

epilepsy, dislocation of kneecap

Suitable for first-time owners

The **ITALIAN GREYHOUND** is an enchanting, gentle, and very affable dog, which must have been the reason why, for centuries, it was the favorite dog of royalty. Catherine the Great had one, as did Queen Victoria, James I of England, and of course, Frederic the Great. Luckily the proximity to such illustrious personages has not spoiled its disposition, and it is still very easy to live with. The Italian Greyhound is one of the most pleasant dogs, peaceful, loving, and well behaved. It looks like a living statue and has, over the centuries, inspired all kinds of artists to depict it. Although it does not need to be walked for hours at a time, it is a greyhound and needs plenty of running to build up its muscles and keep them in shape. It is a very fast runner and likes to show off its skills. The Italian Greyhound is easy to train because it is always eager to please its master. Training in a calm and kind manner does wonders for this dog's self-confidence. The Italian Greyhound naturally tends to be reserved and even somewhat timid toward strangers, with whom it generally wants to have as little to do as possible. For this reason, it is important to socialize it well, starting when it is still a puppy. Graceful, elegant, noble-looking, and definitely practical because its hair is so short, the Italian Greyhound is an ideal apartment dog.

Height	male: approximately 14 in (35 cm); female: approximately 13 in (33 cm)
Weight	9–18 lbs (4–8 kg)
Coat	smooth-haired variety: dense, flat, glossy; wire-haired variety: dense, hard, wiry
Color	base color is white, with brown and/or black markings

The **JACK RUSSELL TERRIER** is a courageous, fast, and tough hunting dog. The English Kennel Club had long and adamantly refused to recognize it as an official breed, but finally relented in 1989, doing so, presumably, because it did not want to miss out on the Jack Russell's growing popularity. This breed, unsurpassed as a hunter of wild boars and a pursuer of vermin and small game in narrow burrows, has meanwhile been recast into a salon dog. It is seen everywhere: in riding stables, on boulevards, at fashion shows, in theater lobbies, and in offices. Yet, the Jack Russell is not a lap dog by nature. It does what it wants to. It is an enthusiastic yapper and a diligent digger of holes. Keeping these dogs in a kennel is not the answer because they become too independent under those conditions. Basic obedience training takes two years, and even after that they still will refuse to obey commands given by other family members. Like most terriers, they are belligerent and always looking for a fight. The males are often sex-obsessed monsters whose lives—not to mention their owners' lives—are made much more peaceful by a castration operation. Anyone who has been fortunate enough to experience a Jack Russell "at his best" becomes a fanatic admirer of the breed. The Jack Russell is always there when anything is happening, merry, comical, and never to be outdone. This dog is filled with incredible energy and is consequently a good match for physically active people, such as marathon runners.

Grooming

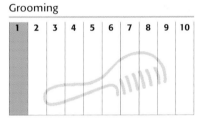

Required Exercise

Suitability for City Living

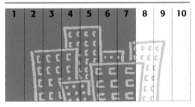

Common Health Problems

For experienced dog owners

JAPANESE CHIN

Height	approximately 10 in (25 cm)
Weight	6 lbs (2.5 kg)
Coat	soft, long
Color	white with regular black or red markings

Grooming

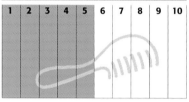

Required Exercise

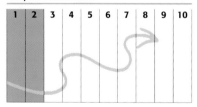

Suitability for City Living

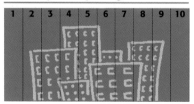

Common Health Problems

respiratory problems, heart attack, dislocation of kneecap

Suitable for first-time owners

The **JAPANESE CHIN** is a perfect apartment dog. It is intelligent, playful, affectionate, and easy to manage. It does shed somewhat and has to be brushed now and then, but its needs for exercise are minimal. The Chin is a lively little dog that wants to be included in everything and is eager to go along, whether it be to a cocktail party, or on any other excursion. This dog never really grows up; it always remains childlike and impertinent enough to draw attention to itself, though it never develops into a household tyrant. The Japanese Chin is fairly delicate, and therefore is not the dog to take part in the wild play of children. What it likes most of all is to be pampered and spoiled, and that is what it was bred for.

Height	male: 18 in (44.5 cm); female: 17 in (42.5 cm)
Weight	55–66 lbs (25–30 kg)
Coat	abundant, hard, guard hair that stands away from body, with a thick undercoat
Color	guard hair a mixture of gray and black; undercoat cream-colored

Grooming

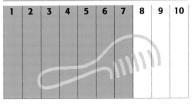

Required Exercise

Suitability for City Living

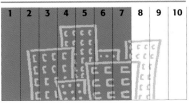

The **KEESHOND** is related to the Samoyed, the Chow Chow, the Norwegian Elkhound, and to dogs of the Spitz family. For a long time, it lived with the boatsmen on Dutch river barges. Today, it is a perfect household companion. It is an attractive, good-humored, easily managed dog with a winning personality and great style. It also smiles—that is, it shows its teeth in a friendly grin. It adapts very eagerly because it craves the proximity of its people, is curious, and doesn't want to miss out on anything. The Keeshond is reserved toward strangers, but quickly makes friends with children. If it has grown up with children, it is incredibly patient with them. This is a lively dog, but if it gets enough exercise it can be kept in the city. The Keeshond is sensitive, but responds well to firm and patient training. Its crowning glory is, of course, its gorgeous coat, which has to be brushed at least twice a week. However, the dog should, if possible, never be bathed because this makes the fur too soft. The Keeshond has a tendency to bark a lot, especially if it is left alone too much.

Common Health Problems

hip dysplasia, heart disease

Suitable for first-time owners

KERRY BLUE TERRIER

Height	19 in (47 cm)
Weight	33–40 lbs (15–18 kg)
Coat	silky soft, very dense, wavy
Color	blue

Grooming

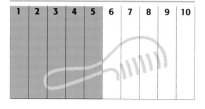

Required Exercise

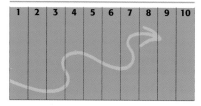

Suitability for City Living

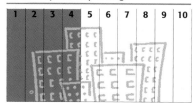

Common Health Problems

For experienced dog owners

The **KERRY BLUE TERRIER** has become a symbol of Ireland, along with the shamrock. This great Irish all-around dog was first bred in the eighteenth century in the County of Kerry as a herding dog. It is equally adept as a watchdog and as a hunting dog that goes after rats in barns, as well as after rabbits and birds. It is also a superb retriever. In Ireland the Kerry Blue is never trimmed, but the English clipped and styled it until it was practically unrecognizable, turning this rugged farm dog into a family dog fit for the living room—almost. The Kerry Blue is a dog of great style and character. It is pugnacious and ebullient, and has not forgotten its original purpose at all. It is not a display dog and usually has no ambitions in that direction. It is not fond of strangers and can be a biter, an urge that must be controlled through very early training. It is a fierce attacker of most other animals, and therefore has to be kept on the leash much of the time. It is also capricious and very strong-willed and will keep trying to outwit its master. It is so stubborn, headstrong, and independent-minded that inexperienced dog owners are likely to have trouble dealing with it. But for a true dog person, the lively, playful Kerry Blue Terrier is a marvelous dog, though it may take a few years of experience before all the problems are ironed out. But anyone who has learned to read the mind of this enigmatic dog will swear by the Kerry Blue.

Height	9–12 in (22–30 cm)
Weight	8–14 lbs (3.5–6.5 kg)
Coat	thick, long, straight, and silky; with abundant feathering on legs
Color	Blenheim variety: white with bright red areas; Prince Charles variety: tricolor; King Charles variety: black with tan; Ruby variety: chestnut-red

The **KING CHARLES SPANIEL** is a lap dog through and through. Happy only if it is near its people, it becomes sad and melancholy if left alone. It barks very little and—unlike its close relative, the Cavalier King Charles—it is indifferent to strangers. Both breeds go back to the same place and time. They were bred in England in the sixteenth century as companion dogs for aristocratic ladies. The less athletic variety, which later came to be known as "King Charles Spaniel," probably was the result of some crossbreeding with Asiatic dogs like the Pug, the Japanese Chin, or the Pekinese. The King Charles Spaniel needs very little exercise, but all the more affection. It is a real people's dog and a true aristocrat, with a will of its own and a deep-seated conviction that obedience training, and the execution of commands, should not be imposed on it.

Grooming

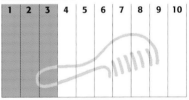

1	2	3	4	5	6	7	8	9	10

Required Exercise

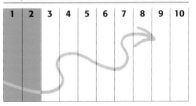

1	2	3	4	5	6	7	8	9	10

Suitability for City Living

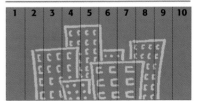

1	2	3	4	5	6	7	8	9	10

Common Health Problems

dislocation of kneecap

Suitable for first-time owners

KLEINER MÜNSTERLÄNDER

Height	20–22 in (52–56 cm)
Weight	approximately 33 lbs (15 kg)
Coat	lying close to the body, medium-long; full feathering on tail; front legs fringed; trousers on back legs
Color	base color brown and white, light or dark roan

Grooming

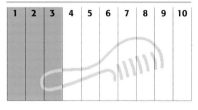

Required Exercise

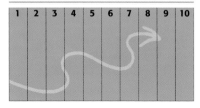

Suitability for City Living

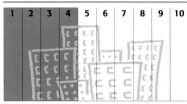

Common Health Problems

entropion, rare hip dysplasia

Suitable for first-time owners

The **KLEINE MÜNSTERLÄNDER** is one of the oldest hunting breeds. It is a superb working dog of great intelligence. Its passion for hunting is indomitable; it never gives in to fatigue, nor is it daunted by the foulest of weather. It follows a scent infallibly and retrieves enthusiastically, points accurately, and loves hunting in water. Being totally devoted to its master, it is easy to train and enjoys lessons. It is also a good watchdog, as well as a reliable, loving friend of children. In addition to having all these useful qualities, it is also a pleasant, very sympathetic companion dog of noble bearing. Because it is so attached to its people, it can even be kept in the city if necessary. But the owner should never forget that this is really a hunting dog that needs very extensive walks throughout its life, as well as things to keep it busy and, if possible, a body of water for swimming.

Height	25 in (63 cm)
Weight	95–99 lbs (43–45 kg)
Coat	dense, weather-resistant double coat consisting of long cords that are matted together
Color	white

The **KOMONDOR** has been raised in Hungary for more than one thousand years. It was originally bred to protect flocks of sheep, which it defended against wolves and bears even in the worst windy and icy cold weather. Very playful as a puppy, the Komondor grows up into a calm and serious dog that likes to act on its own judgment, and therefore has to be well trained and kept under firm control. It is totally unfit for city life. This sturdy, big-boned dog needs a lot of room and likes best being outside. The heavy, corded coat protects it against any weather. The Komondor is a watchdog not to be trifled with; it is very suspicious of strangers and takes its time accepting even those who are obviously friends of the household. Visitors are watched calmly, but with intent alertness, and anyone seeming to pose a threat to the home or its people may be subject to serious attack. The Komondor loves its master and family with boundless loyalty. This dog's coat takes two days to dry out completely after a bath, and taking care of it can be an all-consuming task—and even if it is tended to, the dog still always looks unkempt. The Komondor is tough, rugged, and very protective, and it needs a great deal of exercise. For these reasons, it should really be kept only by people who are able to devote full attention to their dog.

Grooming

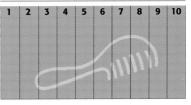

| 1 | 2 | 3 | 4 | 5 | 6 | 7 | 8 | 9 | 10 |

Required Exercise

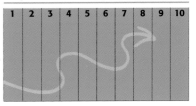

| 1 | 2 | 3 | 4 | 5 | 6 | 7 | 8 | 9 | 10 |

Suitability for City Living

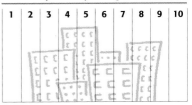

| 1 | 2 | 3 | 4 | 5 | 6 | 7 | 8 | 9 | 10 |

Common Health Problems

hip dysplasia, twisted stomach

For experienced dog owners

KROMFOHRLÄNDER

Height	15-18 in (38–46 cm)
Weight	22–35 lbs (10–16 kg)
Coat	smooth or wire-haired
Color	white with chestnut areas; preferably, ears and sides of head should be chestnut

Grooming

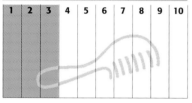

Required Exercise

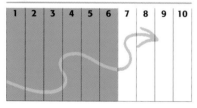

Suitability for City Living

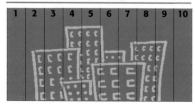

Common Health Problems

arthrosis if overtaxed as a puppy, rarely epilepsy

Suitable for first-time owners

The **KROMFOHRLÄNDER** is a relatively young breed that came about by accident in the 1950s in Germany. It has since been bred deliberately and systematically as a family dog. It is a highly intelligent, cheerful, vivacious, and adaptable companion dog that tends to be a one-man dog. Though it appreciates the rest of the family, it obeys them only when it suits its fancy, and it cannot be recommended as a child's dog without qualifications. The Kromfohrländer doesn't put up with everything, and only should be around children who have learned to respect dogs. For children like that, however, this active dog makes a delightful companion, always ready for adventure and wild play. It is also a good watchdog that detects the slightest sound and likes to bark. Initially distrustful of strangers, it eventually learns to accept them.

The Kromfohrländer likes to run a lot. Consistent training and good early socialization are a must for this dog, which is very intelligent and learns extremely fast. It masters desired behaviors as well as fancy tricks with ease, but it is also good at spotting its owner's weaknesses. If once given a tidbit from the table, it will not stop begging for food for the rest of its life. It is an outstanding agility dog with a good sense of humor. This dog should live with active people who treat it with firm consistency and can appreciate its wit. From such people, it is unlikely to ever do anything amiss.

Height	28–30 in (70–76 cm)
Weight	approximately 114 lbs (52 kg)
Coat	long double coat, somewhat wavy or lying flat to the body
Color	white or ivory

Grooming

1	2	3	4	5	6	7	8	9	10

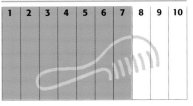

The **KUVASZ** was at one time the darling of the Hungarian aristocrats, among whom intrigue was so prevalent that King Mathias I once said in reference to this breed that he trusted his dogs more than humans. The name "Kuvasz" is originally Turkish and means "protector," a name that accurately describes this beautiful white dog's mission in life. The Kuvasz is said to have an unerring instinct for telling its master's enemies. It is fiercely loyal and protective. People say that this dog is either your friend or your enemy for life. It is a working dog through and through that gets bored easily and needs to be kept busy, or it will get restless and destructive. It can also be aggressive toward other dogs and has to be taught from the time it is a puppy to accept other animals and people. The owner of a Kuvasz has to have some special qualities because this dog likes to think it is smarter than its master—a question that should never be allowed to arise. Anyone wanting to own a Kuvasz has to be calm, strong, experienced, and able to assert his or her own will to be able to manage this stubborn, independent-minded dog. A Kuvasz that is the least bit out of control is not just disagreeable, but potentially dangerous. It is not a dog you can simply keep fenced in the yard; it needs to be close to its people.

Required Exercise

1	2	3	4	5	6	7	8	9	10

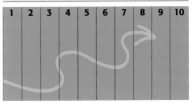

Suitability for City Living

1	2	3	4	5	6	7	8	9	10

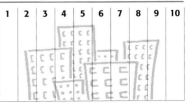

Common Health Problems

hip dysplasia, allergies, eczema

For experienced dog owners

LABRADOR RETRIEVER

Height	male: 22–24 in (55–62 cm); female: 21–24 in (54–60 cm)
Weight	male: 66–79 lbs (30–36 kg); female: 55–70 lbs (25–32 kg)
Coat	hard, dense guard hair with water-repellent undercoat
Color	black, chocolate, yellow

Grooming

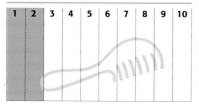

Required Exercise

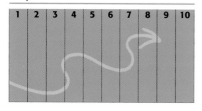

Suitability for City Living

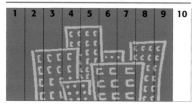

Common Health Problems

hip dysplasia, cataracts, progressive retinal atrophy, epilepsy

Suitable for first-time owners

The **LABRADOR RETRIEVER** was originally pure black and was bred to work in the water, which is why it has a water-repellent coat and webbed feet. It has become one of the most popular companion dogs, especially among owners of sport utility vehicles. It is one of the world's best family dogs and can be kept under almost any conditions because it is so sensitive, adaptable, and imperturbable. It is up to the owner to do right by this wonderful dog; the dog itself will hardly ever assert any demands of its own. However, to keep this dog in a small city apartment without sufficient exercise is unfair and unconscionable, and so is not letting it swim regularly. Labradors were "invented" for the water, and diving for sticks is one of life's requirements for them, regardless of the weather.

The Labrador Retriever is good-natured, willing to learn, and fond of eating. The last trait can be its downfall, for an overfed Labrador is a very dull dog. One that is kept in good trim, on the other hand, is a wonderful playmate for children, an outstanding helper of handicapped or blind people, and a great narcotics detective. It cannot be kept in a kennel because it feels lost without human company, and it is hopeless as a watchdog because distrust has no room in its generous heart. It would be more than happy to show any thief the way to the refrigerator.

Height	approximately 14 in (36 cm)
Weight	male: 17 lbs (7.7 kg); female: 15 lbs (6.8 kg)
Coat	hard, dense, waterproof, with dense, soft undercoat
Color	blue with tan, black and tan, red, wheat, red grizzle, liver, blue, and black

The **LAKELAND TERRIER** is one of the oldest English working terriers and still has a strongly developed hunting instinct. It is absolutely fearless, full of fire, playful, and it never tires. At the same time, it is more reliable than most terriers, quieter, and much more reasonable. The Lakeland is friendly and good-natured, and it gets along beautifully with children it knows. It adores its master, but warms up to strangers only slowly. It seems to have little interest in superficial relationships and responds to people more in an "all or nothing" manner. It is a convenient size, and vigilant, but barks only when necessary. As long as it gets enough walks, play time, and human company, it can be kept in the city without problems. The Lakeland can be incredibly stubborn, and therefore has to be well trained—as do all terriers—but must never be beaten or yanked around. Its coat has to be stripped twice a year. The Lakeland Terrier is a sensitive, pleasant, and highly intelligent family dog that is quite rare and deserves much wider appreciation.

Grooming

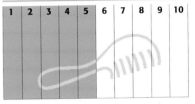

| 1 | 2 | 3 | 4 | 5 | 6 | 7 | 8 | 9 | 10 |

Required Exercise

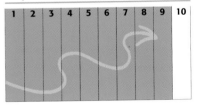

| 1 | 2 | 3 | 4 | 5 | 6 | 7 | 8 | 9 | 10 |

Suitability for City Living

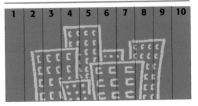

| 1 | 2 | 3 | 4 | 5 | 6 | 7 | 8 | 9 | 10 |

Common Health Problems

Suitable for first-time owners

LANDSEER

Height	26–31 in (67–80 cm)
Weight	132–154 lbs (60–70 kg)
Coat	long, heavy, dense
Color	white base color with black areas; head is always black

Grooming

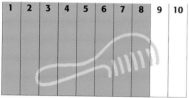

1	2	3	4	5	6	7	8	9	10

Required Exercise

1	2	3	4	5	6	7	8	9	10

Suitability for City Living

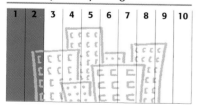

1	2	3	4	5	6	7	8	9	10

Common Health Problems

Suitable for first-time owners

The **LANDSEER** was once a black and white version of the Newfoundland, named after the English painter Sir Edwin Landseer. When the black Newfoundland became fashionable, the Landseer vanished almost completely, and reappeared only as recently as the 1930s, thanks to the efforts of German and Swiss breeders. The result of their work is a dog that is lighter than the Newfoundland and with a less heavy, and easier to care for, coat. The Landseer is still relatively rare, but that is of advantage to the breed's health, as it would be for any breed. It is definitely a family dog that would like best being next to its people, preferably in their lap. It is not a dog that can be bought and then relegated to the yard. An affable, faithful, and good-natured member of the household, it centers all its attention on its people. It is reliable, very intelligent, and easy to train—the latter a welcome trait in a dog of this size. The Landseer has an excellent nose and is a first-class retriever both on land and in the water. Some individuals have an urge to hunt, but early training can reliably keep this hunting instinct under control. The Landseer cannot be kept in an apartment. It needs a large outdoor area, preferably with some children playing there whom it can watch and protect. It also needs walks and—unless you live on the beach—regular opportunities for swimming. Because this dog grows very fast, it is important to know its nutritional requirements and feed it accordingly.

Height	30–31 in (76–80 cm)
Weight	more than 88 lbs (40 kg)
Coat	moderately long, dense, medium-soft, waterproof
Color	sand, light yellow, gold, or chestnut; always with a black mask

Grooming

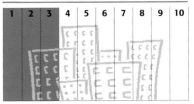

| 1 | 2 | 3 | 4 | 5 | 6 | 7 | 8 | 9 | 10 |

Required Exercise

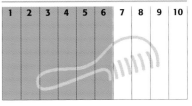

| 1 | 2 | 3 | 4 | 5 | 6 | 7 | 8 | 9 | 10 |

Suitability for City Living

| 1 | 2 | 3 | 4 | 5 | 6 | 7 | 8 | 9 | 10 |

The **LEONBERGER** is a noble and gentle giant. It is the creation of one Heinrich Essig, city councillor of Leonberg, Germany, who wanted to obtain a dog that resembled the lion in the city's coat-of-arms. To establish the breed, he crossed the Saint Bernard, the Landseer, and the Great Pyrenees, but he kept the exact "recipe" of the mix a secret. The Leonberger is a delightful dog, friendly, easy to handle, patient, reliable, perhaps a little too serious, but with a charming and generous personality. It is quiet and restrained indoors, but lively and playful outdoors, with boundless energy. Although it adores its master as well as the other members of the family and, in order to please them, tries to adapt to whatever the situation may be, this dog really should be kept only in a rural setting where there is room enough for running, and preferably swimming. The Leonberger is relatively outgoing toward strangers, although at about three years of age, when it has reached full maturity, it becomes somewhat more discriminating—though never aggressive—in its dealings with unfamiliar people. (Luckily, the average thief is unaware of the dog's restraint.) The Landseer is always willing to cooperate, easy to train, and incredibly patient with small children. Its coat requires little care, but its big, hairy paws track lots of mud and sand into the house. On the other hand, it does not drool.

Common Health Problems

hip dysplasia, eyelid abnormalities

Suitable for first-time owners

LHASA APSO

Height	approximately 10 in (25 cm)
Weight	approximately 13–22 lbs (6–10 kg)
Coat	long, heavy, straight, and fairly hard; with a moderately thick undercoat
Color	all colors, including multicolored

Grooming

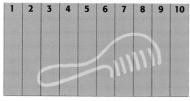

1	2	3	4	5	6	7	8	9	10

Required Exercise

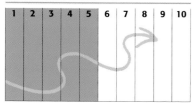

1	2	3	4	5	6	7	8	9	10

Suitability for City Living

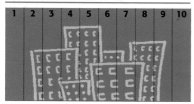

1	2	3	4	5	6	7	8	9	10

The **LHASA APSO** was originally kept by Buddhist monks to act as sentinel of their monasteries. It was also a bringer of good luck and was presented as such by the Dalai Lhama to specially chosen recipients. On account of this, the Lhasa Apso has been treated with great seriousness and respect for centuries—an attitude this dog expects from those around it in the modern Western world, too. The Lhasa is a very self-confident, lively dog that loves its family, but is suspicious of strangers—a quality that dates back to its days as a Tibetan watchdog. But once it has had a chance to become acquainted with the newcomers, it is outgoing and without a trace of aggression. The Lhasa Apso is a small dog with a big personality, independent, and strong-minded. It is a demanding dog that definitely is no lap dog and doesn't want to be one. It is not ideal around small children because it is not particularly patient, and doesn't put up with being mauled. The owner has to establish clearly from the beginning who is in charge, or else the Lhasa Apso can turn into a full-fledged despot. Yet, it is playful and loving at heart and accepts training happily. In recent years, this dog has become very popular, and it is therefore important to find a good, conscientious breeder if you want to buy a puppy.

Common Health Problems

hip dysplasia, liver disease

Suitable for first-time owners

Height	13 in (32 cm)
Weight	11 lbs (5 kg)
Coat	long, wavy, silky soft, but with body
Color	any color or color combination

The **LÖWCHEN** is convinced that life is delightful. Perhaps this cheerful attitude derives from being allowed for centuries to sleep on the beds of ladies—as a kind of living hot-water bottle—and spending the rest of its time, shorn lion-fashion, being petted and fussed over by its female owner. Although the Löwchen looks like a luxury pet, it has the stuff to withstand all the storms of life. The breed is intelligent and smart as a whip; it is also extremely healthy and has preserved its good instincts in spite of considerable inbreeding resulting from its rareness. The Löwchen has the reputation of being especially vigilant, and has to be trained early not to turn into a yapper. It is very playful and so good with children that it easily lets itself be manhandled. It is very athletic and loves walks, though it doesn't absolutely have to have them, and is satisfied with playing in the yard. Because these dogs are so irresistibly cute as puppies, the owner may find it hard to be hard-nosed about training. Very clever at finding ways not to obey, the Löwchen is a master at charming everyone around it into letting it have its way, but it readily submits to firm training. This dog has to be combed regularly. Whether it is shorn is up to the owner's taste, but it should never be deprived of its fur in temperatures when we would be uncomfortable wearing shorts.

Grooming

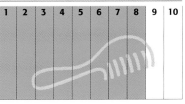

1	2	3	4	5	6	7	8	9	10

Required Exercise

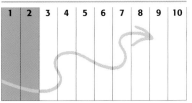

1	2	3	4	5	6	7	8	9	10

Suitability for City Living

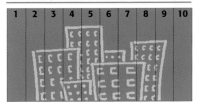

1	2	3	4	5	6	7	8	9	10

Common Health Problems

bad teeth, dislocation of kneecap

Suitable for first-time owners

MALTESE

Height	8–10 in (20–25 cm)
Weight	4–7 lbs (1.8–3 kg)
Coat	long, silky, abundant
Color	pure white

Grooming

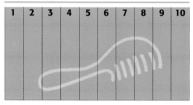

Required Exercise

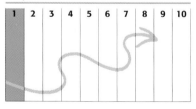

Suitability for City Living

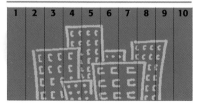

Common Health Problems

eye infections, gingivitis, spinal problems

Suitable for first-time owners

The **MALTESE** is probably one of the world's oldest dog breeds. It was a favorite of the upper classes in ancient Rome and Greece and, in the time of Elizabeth I, the steady companion of well-born English ladies. Even five hundred years ago these dogs commanded huge sums, the equivalent of the yearly income of a whole village of workers.

The Maltese is in many ways like a child, a fact that potential owners should keep in mind. It is loving, full of personality, playful, intelligent, and adores its master. But it can be a fussy eater with a complicated digestive system. And, of course, its gorgeous coat requires constant attention. The Maltese can be quite delicate and likes to be warm and dry, though it also wants daily walks. Its dreams are more of velvet cushions than of flocks of sheep. After all, it was bred to be a lap dog two thousand years ago, and by now this has become imprinted in its genes. The Maltese can be pert and unfriendly toward strangers, and even toward people it knows, and it is therefore important to get it used to unfamiliar persons, and different surroundings, from the time it is a puppy.

Height	28–30 in (70–76 cm)
Weight	175–190 lbs (80–85 kg)
Coat	short, hard
Color	fawn, apricot, or brindle; with a black mask and darker ears

Grooming

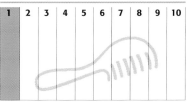

Required Exercise

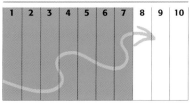

Suitability for City Living

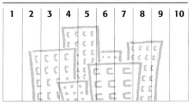

Common Health Problems

hip dysplasia, entropion, thyroid malfunctioning, bladder problems

For experienced dog owners

The **MASTIFF** is among dogs what the lion is among wild animals. In spite of its huge size, it is a wonderful family dog, good-natured, loving, even-tempered, and very fond of children. It belongs in a rural setting because, given its size, it needs a lot of space and opportunity for walking and running—whether its seems to want to exercise or not. It also needs the proximity of its people, and therefore cannot simply be relegated to the yard. As a rule, it is obedient by nature and thus easy to train, taking very seriously whatever it is asked to do. Training should be accompanied by lots of praise and very little correction. A Mastiff should never be hit. It should be well socialized with people and other animals from early on so that it develops an accurate sense of its own size. Most Mastiffs are friendly toward strangers, and that is just as well. Dogs generally can tell on their own, and without special training, if there is any danger. A Mastiff should never be allowed to become aggressive; its size alone is enough to deter just about anyone trying to break in. The Mastiff's coat needs practically no care, but this dog does drool constantly.

NEOPOLITAN MASTIFF

Height	24–30 in (60–75 cm)
Weight	up to 154 lbs (70 kg)
Coat	short, thick, shiny
Color	bluish-gray, black, brown, reddish-yellow, fawn, brindle

Grooming

1	2	3	4	5	6	7	8	9	10

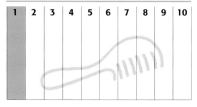

Required Exercise

1	2	3	4	5	6	7	8	9	10

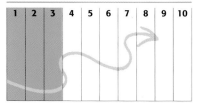

Suitability for City Living

1	2	3	4	5	6	7	8	9	10

Common Health Problems

hip dysplasia, entropion, ectropion

For experienced dog owners

The **NEOPOLITAN MASTIFF** is a direct descendent of the Roman Molossian dogs. It was used to fight in wars and in gladiatorial contests. It also served as a draft animal, companion, and guard dog. In spite of its fear-inspiring appearance, it is a faithful, quiet, and affectionate companion and a child's playmate of truly stoic patience. It loves its master and his or her friends, and barks only when it thinks the situation really requires it. The Neopolitan is a dog of huge bulk, and therefore not for people of limited physical strength. Nor is it the right dog for very athletic dog lovers because it is slow and bearlike in its movements and reluctant to change its deliberate pace. It needs at least an hour of exercise a day, even if it doesn't seem to want it. It is important not to let this mastiff get obese since it is very bad for its health, as it is for all breeds. Respectful and consistent subordination training is essential, or you will lose all control over this phenomenally strong dog. It must never be allowed to become aggressive or trained as a guard dog. Its mere presence is impressive enough to scare any intruder away. An aggressive Neopolitan, like any other very large dog, is truly a danger to life and limb.

Height	26–28 in (65–70 cm)
Weight	99–150 lbs (45–68 kg)
Coat	long, heavy, shiny, lying flat to the body, slightly wavy
Color	black, brown

Grooming

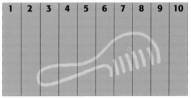

Required Exercise

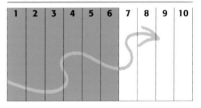

Suitability for City Living

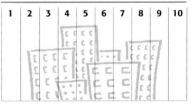

The **NEWFOUNDLAND** is a giant among dogs, but in looks and personality resembles a teddy bear. Its origins have given rise to endless speculation, but nothing definite is known about its ancestry. One likely theory holds that it is descended from Tibetan Mastiffs. In Newfoundland, it was kept as a working dog expected to haul in nets, pull carts, and carry heavy loads. In addition to all that, it also acquired legendary fame for rescuing people from the water. Today, though, the Newfoundland is primarily an irresistible family dog. It is reserved, but pleasant, toward unfamiliar people and becomes very friendly once it feels that a stranger poses no threat to the family. Although not mistrustful by nature, the Newfoundland is very protective, a trait that should be kept in mind with a dog of its size. A Newfoundland should never be trained as a guard dog; its mere bulk is enough to deter the most determined thief. The Newfoundland is very outgoing and even-tempered, and thus an ideal family member that patiently lets children climb all over it and even puts up with having toys stuck in its ears. The only thing this dog cannot tolerate is a lack of human affection.

The Newfoundland was bred to work in the water, as is evident in its webbed feet. To keep it from swimming because it might get the house wet and dirty borders on cruelty. Some drawbacks to owning this dog are that its coat needs time-consuming grooming, in bad weather it carts loads of dirt into the house, and it drools quite a lot.

Common Health Problems

hip dysplasia, eyelid abnormalities, heart disease

Suitable for first-time owners

NORFOLK TERRIER

Height	10 in (25 cm)
Weight	11 lbs (5 kg)
Coat	hard, wiry, straight, lying flat to the body, with short, dense undercoat
Color	red, wheaten, black and tan, grizzle

Grooming

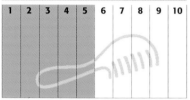

Required Exercise

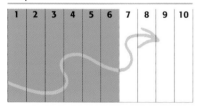

Suitability for City Living

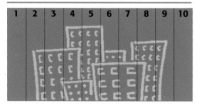

Common Health Problems

cramps, breathing problems, epilepsy

Suitable for first-time owners

The **NORFOLK TERRIER** has the same origins as the Norwich Terrier. Both were working breeds, tough little ratters. In 1964 they were recognized as two separate breeds that differ from each other more than just in the shape of their ears, which droop in the Norfolk but are pricked in its cousin. The Norfolk Terrier is one of the smallest terriers as measured by the height at the withers, but one of the largest in terms of personality. It is incredibly adaptable to both its physical and human environment, playing whatever role is expected of it—anything from one-man dog to family clown—as long as it gets enough exercise and is kept busy. The Norfolk is very curious and active, and always wants to be included in whatever is happening. It takes readily to training—this in itself sets it apart from most other terriers—and considers obedience lessons the most entertaining way imaginable to pass time. Because of its acute hearing, the Norfolk is used as a therapy dog for hearing-impaired people. With its irresistible charm, it quickly wins the hearts of all around it. The Norfolk is small and manageable enough to be taken along on travels; it is also very self-confident and adjusts well to new situations. It is an alert little watchdog without being a yapper, has relatively little urge to hunt, and is not at all belligerent. Its hard coat rarely gets really dirty, but the dog's fur does have to be trimmed twice a year. However, a Norfolk Terrier should never be shorn; that makes its coat too soft.

Height	10–12 in (25–30 cm)
Weight	11 lbs (5 kg)
Coat	hard, wiry, straight, lying flat to the body, with short, dense undercoat
Color	red, wheaten, black and tan, grizzle

Grooming

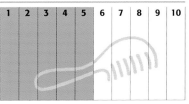

Required Exercise

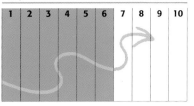

Suitability for City Living

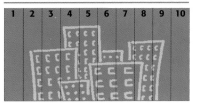

Common Health Problems

minor heart abnormalities, breathing problems

Suitable for first-time owners

The **NORWICH TERRIER** is closely related to the Norfolk Terrier and was not recognized as a separate breed until 1964. It has small pricked ears, unlike its cousin. It is one of the smallest terriers, but has an impressive personality. It is everything a terrier should be: hardy, courageous, cheerful, honest, full of fire, self-confident, yet also very agreeable, loyal, easy to teach, and without any aggression or nervousness. It was bred to adjust to any situation and is an ideal small family dog that loves adventure and excitement, always wants to be part of everything, and considers it its job to entertain and delight everyone around it. It needs walks and things to do, but is easy to train because it thinks lessons with its master are great fun; thus, it is always ready to learn any trick. Its coat requires little care and is relatively dirt-resistant, but the dog does have to be trimmed twice a year—trimmed, not shorn, or its fur will get too soft. The Norwich Terrier is an ideal dog no matter what your living situation. The only thing it can't tolerate is lack of attention and affection. The Norwich is utterly dependent on its people.

OLD ENGLISH SHEEPDOG

Height	22–23 in (56–58 cm)
Weight	66 lbs (30 kg)
Coat	thick, soft, long-haired
Color	any shade of gray or blue, with white markings

Grooming

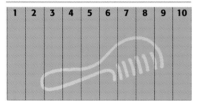

Required Exercise

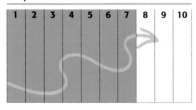

Suitability for City Living

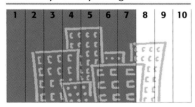

Common Health Problems

hip dysplasia, skin problems

For experienced dog owners

The **OLD ENGLISH SHEEPDOG**, or **BOBTAIL**, is a good-natured, loyal, affable, and peace-loving dog. It is upbeat and enthusiastic without being wild, loves children, and is basically obedient. At the same time, it is obstinate and sensitive, and the adult dog will show in its character how it was raised. A Bobtail that did not get enough physical exercise, was left alone too much, and was yanked around while being trained will grow up into an uncontrollable, destructive troublemaker. Originally bred to herd sheep, the English Sheepdog has caught on more recently as a watchdog and a fashionable pet. Its problem is that it is irresistibly cute as a puppy, looking just like a fluffy little ball of fur. The phase of huge popularity the Bobtail experienced took its toll on the breed, as it always does in such cases. Breeders of doubtful ethics cashed in on the Bobtail boom and turned out puppies as fast as they could, without paying attention to the wonderful, even-tempered nature of this breed. As a result, many miserable, timid, or aggressive Bobtails came on the market and ultimately ended up in animal shelters after they lost their cute puppy look. Don't be fooled by the teddy-bear-like looks of this dog. It is a working dog that needs plenty of space and exercise and has to be trained patiently. But if you devote enough time and attention to the Bobtail from the very beginning, you will have a steady and utterly loyal companion no matter what the circumstances of your life are.

Height	8–11 in (20–29 cm)
Weight	9–10 lbs (4–4.5 kg)
Coat	profuse, fine, silky; ears and hind legs well feathered, with a thick ruff
Color	mostly white with patches of any color; also liver or tricolor

The **PAPILLON** is not a lap dog by nature, even though it has been depicted as a "lady's dog" in many portraits of high-born ladies ever since the sixteenth century, and was Marie Antoinette's favorite pet dog. From the French word for "butterfly" the Papillon's ears supposedly resemble the shape of a butterfly. The Papillon is much more rugged than it looks. This toy spaniel is very intelligent and high-spirited; it is an expert catcher of rats and has the makings of a superb agility dog. It is as happy in the country as in the city. If treated as a regular dog, it is outgoing and self-confident; if spoiled and pampered, it easily becomes nervous, timid, and unsure of itself. In spite of its elegant appearance, it loves long walks and adventures of all kinds, and therefore is a good traveling companion that adjusts to any climate and all kinds of circumstances. The Papillon is quiet and loving, learns tricks easily, and gets along well with other pets. It is affectionate, obeys members of the family readily, and is also a very good little watchdog.

Grooming

1	2	3	4	5	6	7	8	9	10

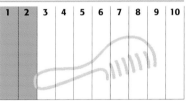

Required Exercise

1	2	3	4	5	6	7	8	9	10

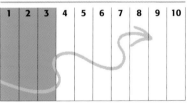

Suitability for City Living

1	2	3	4	5	6	7	8	9	10

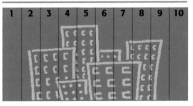

Common Health Problems

tends to sustain fractures (don't allow it to jump off furniture)

Suitable for first-time owners

PEKINGESE

Height	approximately 7 in (18 cm)
Weight	10–13 lbs (4.5–6 kg)
Coat	long, straight, profuse, with a pronounced mane around the neck
Color	all colors are permitted except liver; always with a black mask

Grooming

1	2	3	4	5	6	7	8	9	10

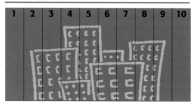

Required Exercise

1	2	3	4	5	6	7	8	9	10

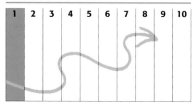

Suitability for City Living

1	2	3	4	5	6	7	8	9	10

Common Health Problems

bladder stones, eye infections, shortness of breath, prolapsed eyeball, jaw problems, cleft palate

Suitable for first-time owners

Legend has it that the **PEKINGESE** came into being when a lion fell in love with a monkey in ancient China and asked a holy man to somehow fit his size to that of his beloved. The result of that happy union was the imperial Pekingese, which was bred and spoiled from then on in the chambers of Chinese palaces. Any attempt to introduce these dogs to the outside world was punished by death. Around 1860, some English officers managed to get their hands on five Pekingese and brought them to England. One of these Pekingese became Queen Victoria's favorite pet dog.

The Pekingese, then, is a dog fit for palaces, and even the dearth of palaces in the modern-day world has done nothing to change its self-image. The Pekingese is a dignified little dog, reserved, proud, affectionate, and displaying a lion's courage whenever the doorbell rings. It is not a dog to play with, and it can get ill-tempered, which is why it is not good around children. The Pekingese is headstrong and stubborn, yet at the same time very sensitive, a combination that makes training practically impossible. Luckily it behaves well on its own. Once it has decided who its master is, that lucky person has a delightful friend and companion. After all, independence, courage, and pride are the qualities we admire in lions.

Height	10–12 in (25.4–30.5 cm)
Weight	22–26.4 lbs (10–12 kg)
Coat	short, hard, dense; with a weatherproof undercoat
Color	red, brown, fawn, black and tan; solid-colored or with white markings

Grooming

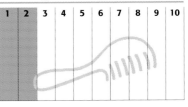

The history of the **PEMBROKE WELSH CORGI** is very different from that of the Cardigan Welsh Corgi. When Henry I brought Flemish weavers to England in the year 1107, this small dog accompanied the immigrants to Wales and herded their cattle there. Unlike the Cardigan, the Pembroke Welsh Corgi has pointed ears and a very short tail. It is a friendly, gentle, even-tempered dog that is equally happy on a farm or in a city apartment. A loving dog, it nevertheless makes a good watchdog that is never belligerent or sneaky. The Pembroke has the heart and the dignity of a big dog and is about as perfect as a dog can get. It has spunk and charm, is obedient by nature, extremely hardy, not too big to take on trips, and so pleasant to have around that one can really take it along anywhere. This dog grows quite old, living not infrequently to the age of 15, 16, or even 17. The Pembroke is a little calmer and more serious than the Cardigan Welsh Corgi, and is a little less accepting of unfamiliar people and dogs. The royal family of England always has several Pembroke Welsh Corgis, and what is good enough for the Windsors is good enough for the rest of us.

Required Exercise

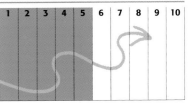

Suitability for City Living

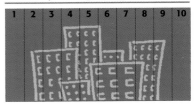

Common Health Problems

Suitable for first-time owners

PHARAOH HOUND

Height	male: 23–25 in (58–63 cm); female: 21–24 in (53–61 cm)
Weight	44–55 lbs (20–25 kg)
Coat	short, glossy, smooth
Color	all colors ranging from bright tan to chestnut, with various white markings

Grooming

1	2	3	4	5	6	7	8	9	10

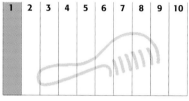

Required Exercise

1	2	3	4	5	6	7	8	9	10

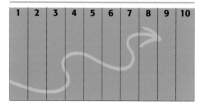

Suitability for City Living

1	2	3	4	5	6	7	8	9	10

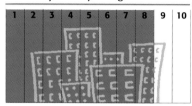

Common Health Problems

Suitable for first-time owners

The **PHARAOH HOUND** goes back to before 3,000 B.C. and was originally bred in Egypt for hunting gazelles. It was owned by members of the wealthy Egyptian upper class and was buried alongside its owner. In our time, it is purely a companion dog of great beauty. Its statuesque elegance reminds us that this dog was in fact the model for the Egyptians' image of the god Anubis. The Pharaoh Hound hunts by sight and smell and is extraordinarily fast and alert. It runs with free, flowing motions, head raised high.

The Pharaoh Hound is affable and loving, very playful, and so intelligent that one can't help but take notice of it. It wants to be close to its people—which is unusual in greyhounds—and insists on being part of—and in the middle of—whatever is happening. The Pharaoh Hound can't stand being left out and makes sure it is involved in everything. It is, of course, a very decorative animal, but it asks much more of life than just being decorative. In fact, it wants to run everybody's life. However, it is easy to train even though it has a strong hunting instinct. As long as it is not handled roughly, it enjoys its lessons because it would do just about anything to please its master. Then too, obedience lessons offer one more opportunity to be the exclusive center of attention.

Height	16–19 in (40–48 cm)
Weight	24–35 lbs (11–16 kg)
Coat	short, hard, shiny, close to the body
Color	pure black, black with tan markings, chestnut to stag red, brown, chocolate, blue-gray with red or yellow markings, salt and pepper

Grooming

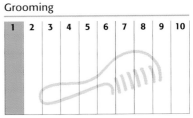

Required Exercise

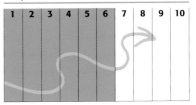

Suitability for City Living

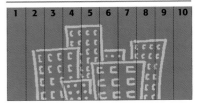

The **PINSCHER** is a very old breed, depicted in many old paintings, and was so common on farms in Germany, where it was used to kill rats, that nobody paid much attention to it. It was not until dog shows became popular at the end of the nineteenth century that a standard was established for it. The name "Pinscher" derives from the English "to pinch," but this dog is anything but a biter. It is a near-perfect companion dog whose coat requires practically no care. It does bark ferociously and is always alert as a watchdog. Highly intelligent, affectionate, devoted, and lively, it is easy to train as long as it is dealt with patiently, lovingly, and fairly. Its elegant looks are reminiscent of the Doberman, which was in fact developed long after the Pinscher. The Pinscher is a thoughtful dog—and therefore excellent at solving problems—and very mistrustful of strangers. For this reason, it has to be well socialized from the beginning. It is also athletic, requiring a lot of exercise, and has the makings of an excellent agility dog. A Pinscher, by the way, is an ideal dog for accompanying a horseback rider on extensive rides; its minimal hunting instinct is easily kept in check. The Pinscher is rare and deserves to become better known. It is reliable and as close to perfect in terms of character, seriousness, size, and ease of care as a dog can get.

Common Health Problems

Suitable for first-time owners

PODENCO IBICENCO

Height	male: 24–26 in (60–66 cm); female: 22–25 in (57–63 cm)
Weight	male: approximately 50 lbs (22.5 kg); female: approximately 42 lbs (9 kg)
Coat	smooth, hard, dense, lying flat to the body; short-haired or wire-haired
Color	red, red and white, or "lionlike" red; feet, tip of tail, chest, muzzle, and facial blaze white

Grooming

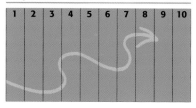

Required Exercise

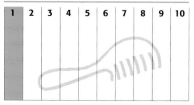

Suitability for City Living

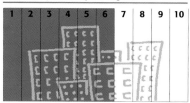

Common Health Problems

Suitable for first-time owners

The **PODENCO IBICENCO** goes back thousands of years, but has recently been encountered in greater numbers primarily on the Balearic Islands. It belongs to the greyhound group and therefore requires a great deal of physical activity. If that can be supplied in the city, it can be kept there because it is extremely clean and quiet indoors. Outdoors, however, this dignified and graceful dog moves with incredible speed and agility, leaps very high from a standing position, and has a rather pronounced hunting instinct. Like most of its relatives, it hunts by sight. Anyone wishing to own a Podenco Ibicenco has to keep in mind that this dog is primarily an athlete, and a fairly large one at that. It can't simply be left in a small apartment. A trustworthy friend of its family, it is relatively friendly toward strangers; but it knows precisely how far its family's territory extends, and no one should try to enter the house without having been greeted by a member of the household. The Podenco Ibicenco has a strong will of its own, and therefore requires firm but very calm and gentle obedience training, starting when it is a puppy. If the same lessons get repeated too much, the Ibicenco quickly gets bored, and it reacts badly to being disciplined or punished.

Height	male: 25–28 in (63–71 cm); female: 23–26 in (58–66 cm)
Weight	44–70 lbs (20–32 kg)
Coat	fine, short, shiny, lying flat to the body
Color	liver, orange, black, or lemon, all in combination with white; solid-colored dogs are very rare

Grooming

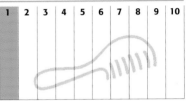

Required Exercise

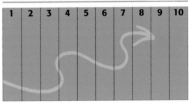

Suitability for City Living

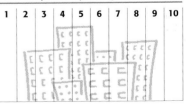

The **POINTER** is the hunting dog we find depicted in paintings since about 1650. It is probably the oldest of all the pointing breeds. It is a powerful, hardy, dignified, and truly charming dog, an aristocrat among sporting breeds. If it is kept as a pet from the time it is a puppy, it makes a wonderful member of the family, patient with children, obedient, and very eager to please its master. At the same time, however, the Pointer is a powerhouse of energy, needs vast amounts of physical activity, and is therefore totally unfit for life in the city. A Pointer that is kept cooped up practically explodes when it is finally let outdoors. There is hardly a more beautiful sight than a Pointer at work, nostrils wide open sniffing for scent of game, tail out straight and horizontal, the whole dog poised motionless and concentrating. The Pointer is a dog for hunters, and if it has a hunter for a master, it is steady and even-tempered in the home. Having been bred for centuries to be the perfect dog for bird hunting, adjustment to a different lifestyle is extremely difficult for it.

Common Health Problems

hip dysplasia, thyroid problems

For experienced dog owners

POODLE

Height	toy: 10 in (25 cm); miniature: 11–14 in (28–35 cm); medium: 14–18 in (35–45 cm); standard: 18–23 in (45–58 cm)
Weight	toy: up to 11 lbs (5 kg); miniature: 15 lbs (7 kg); medium: 26 lbs (12 kg); standard: 48 lbs (22 kg)
Coat	double coat, profuse, woolly, very curly
Color	black, white, brown, silver, apricot

Grooming

1	2	3	4	5	6	7	8	9	10

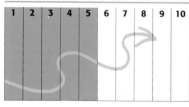

Required Exercise

1	2	3	4	5	6	7	8	9	10

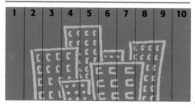

Suitability for City Living

1	2	3	4	5	6	7	8	9	10

Common Health Problems

hip dysplasia, progressive retinal atrophy, epilepsy, skin problems, twisted stomach (in the standard size), tendency to develop cataracts

Suitable for first-time owners

The **POODLE** is a wonderful dog. It can't help it if people clip it into ridiculous shapes, nor can it help being doted on too much. A long time ago, before the invention of mechanical clippers, the Poodle was an excellent hunting and water dog. The word "poodle" derives from the old German "Pfudel," or "Pfütze" in modern German, which means "puddle." Initially the Poodle was clipped a little so that it could work in the water more easily. Then it became very popular among French aristocrats, and this popularity has spread to all classes worldwide. The secret of this popularity is probably the Poodle's intelligence. Clipped or unclipped, and of whatever size, the Poodle is probably the smartest of all dogs. It is also a tireless clown, reliable, loyal, easy to train, willing to learn not only any trick you care to teach it, but also a few of its own. It is an unsurpassed children's dog that is willing to listen for hours to adolescent jokes, or let itself be dressed up in the most outlandish costumes (being used to looking ridiculous after centuries of wearing the pompom of the continental clip). Finally, it is also a very active and athletic dog. There is nothing a Poodle can't or won't learn. It has very acute hearing and an excellent sense of orientation. Problems arise only if force is used in training, or if it is spoiled too much. Then it can easily become obstinate and resentful. But if it is treated like the tough, intelligent dog it is, it has practically no weaknesses. (This may not be true of the Toy Poodle, whose personality and brain capacity seem to have shrunk along with its size.)

Height	24–26 in (60–65 cm)
Weight	55–77 lbs (25–35 kg)
Coat	medium-long, wiry, hard
Color	liver

Grooming

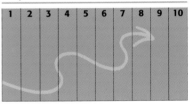

1	2	3	4	5	6	7	8	9	10

The **POODLE POINTER** is a rare German hunting breed that was developed at the end of the nineteenth century by crossing Pointers, Standard Poodles, and almost certainly German Wire-haired Pointers. In fact, the Poodle Pointer looks so much like the last-named breed that the two are hard to tell apart. The Poodle Pointer is very versatile. It is a runner and retriever that is willing to work at any temperature, and, not surprisingly given its Poodle blood, it is also a passionate water dog. Its specialties are partridge, marsh birds, and wild rabbits. The Poodle Pointer is very lively, perhaps a little more light-hearted than its wire-haired cousin, and definitely energetic and intelligent. It takes its job very seriously and doesn't like wasting its time on other things. That is why only hunters should own this dog. This by no means implies, however, that the Poodle Pointer is not a nice dog to have around the house; it is, but it should have a master who is an active and devoted hunter.

Required Exercise

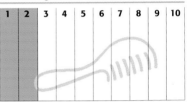

1	2	3	4	5	6	7	8	9	10

Suitability for City Living

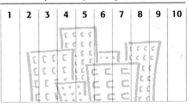

1	2	3	4	5	6	7	8	9	10

Common Health Problems

rare hip dysplasia

For experienced dog owners

PUG

Height	approximately 10–12 in (25–30 cm)
Weight	from 14–18 lbs (6.3–8 kg)
Coat	smooth, dense, glossy, soft
Color	silver, black, beige; with a black mask

Grooming

1	2	3	4	5	6	7	8	9	10

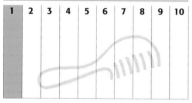

Required Exercise

1	2	3	4	5	6	7	8	9	10

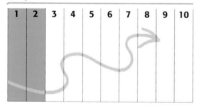

Suitability for City Living

1	2	3	4	5	6	7	8	9	10

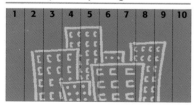

Common Health Problems

spondylosis, dislocation of kneecap, keratitis, demodex

Suitable for first-time owners

The **PUG** is not what we think of as an ordinary dog, and this is obvious at first glance. This dog is only for people who don't mind if their best friend snores, grunts, sheds, and invariably claims the most comfortable spot on the sofa. The Pug is in a class all its own. It has a split personality. Its face looks as though it carried all the world's woes on its shoulders, but the eyes are full of fire. At times it is calm and friendly, at others wild, playful, and filled with amazing athletic spirit.

The Pug probably originated in China. It has the pushed-in face and ring tail that the Chinese valued so highly in their palace dogs. Genghis Khan supposedly brought the dog to Europe. At any rate, it had appeared there by the seventeenth century and became the pet dog of the nobility, of snobs, and of old maids. Contrary to common prejudices, the Pug is not stupid, fat, and clumsy, but rather an ideal small companion that does not smell or slobber, is easy to handle, and generally responds well to basic obedience training. Keeping the Pug from doing something it has set its mind on does, however, require considerable firmness and persistence. This is an intelligent and cheerful dog that loves children, adjusts to whatever situation it finds itself in, and feels just as happy in a small apartment as in a country manor. It is content with a walk of half an hour, but can easily keep going for five hours. It doesn't snap, but does snore frightfully. The Pug has always had just one mission in life: to be loved, and that mission it fulfills brilliantly.

Height	male: 17 in (43 cm); female: 16 in (40.5 cm)
Weight	29–33 lbs (13–15 kg)
Coat	corded; i.e., long, thin strings and felt-like mats cover the entire body
Color	solid black, rust-red, gray, or white

Grooming

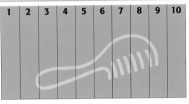

1	2	3	4	5	6	7	8	9	10

Required Exercise

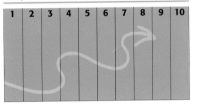

1	2	3	4	5	6	7	8	9	10

Suitability for City Living

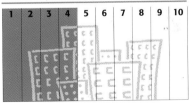

1	2	3	4	5	6	7	8	9	10

Common Health Problems

rare retinal dysplasia

For experienced dog owners

The **PULI** is one of the great Hungarian herding dogs, an expert at a job it has been doing for more than a thousand years. It is an agile, very active dog that has lost none of its herding instinct. Tough and highly intelligent, the Puli has to be well trained by someone who knows exactly what training means. This is not a dog for an indifferent owner who acquired a dog without thought to what this step entails. The Puli is not just reserved toward strangers, but positively mistrustful, a quality that makes it a first-class watchdog. But this instinct has to be kept under firm control, so that vigilance does not turn into aggression.

The Puli is obviously a special dog designed for special tasks. Its coat also sets it apart from other breeds and would be a nightmare for any overly neat housewife. It mats together in long strings, protecting the dog against any weather, but also carrying all manner of dirt and rubbish into the house from outside. The Puli is probably more than anyone who has not owned a dog before can handle. Unless the owner has firm control of this dog, can appreciate its qualities, and is able to challenge its extraordinary capacity to learn, the Puli is not only wasted, but will become a troublesome imposition. This breed is headstrong, self-confident, and an expert in its field of activity, which is to guard its master's land and keep other animals in check. The Puli is reputed to be one of the most intelligent dogs anywhere.

PYRENEES SHEEPDOG

Height	male: 16–20 in (40–50 cm); female: 15–20 in (38–50 cm)
Weight	approximately 31–40 lbs (14–18 kg)
Coat	long and coarse, very thick and somewhat wavy; something between goat's hair and sheep's wool
Color	all shades of gray or dun, with or without brindle or tiger stripes; solid color or with minor white mottle

Grooming

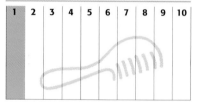

1	2	3	4	5	6	7	8	9	10

Required Exercise

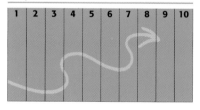

1	2	3	4	5	6	7	8	9	10

Suitability for City Living

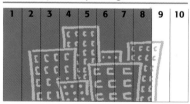

1	2	3	4	5	6	7	8	9	10

The **PYRENEES SHEEPDOG** is thought to be the oldest French sheepdog. The breed was developed in the Pyrenean Mountains, where the Berger's task was to keep the sheep together in a flock while other, mastiff-like dogs defended them against wild animals. The Pyrenees Sheepdog is self-assured, full of energy, bold, lively, and extremely intelligent. It should be kept as a family dog only if it is given work to do; otherwise it will turn into a hyperactive nuisance. The Pyrenees is very alert and agile, reacting to the slightest sound, and consequently tends to bark a lot. However, the barking can be kept within reasonable bounds if the dog is trained early and thoroughly enough. This is an extremely hardy dog. It requires very little grooming and is uncomplicated, as long as it gets enough physical exercise and has some work to keep it busy.

Common Health Problems

Suitable for first-time owners

Height	male: up to 27 in (69 cm); female: 24–26 in (61–66 cm)
Weight	male: 75 lbs (33.9 kg); female: 65 lbs (29.4 kg)
Coat	short, dense, sleek, glossy
Color	wheaten yellow to fox-red

Grooming

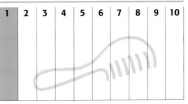

Required Exercise

Suitability for City Living

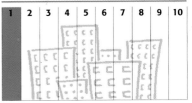

The **RHODESIAN RIDGEBACK** is named for a unique physical feature the breed has, namely, a ridge running down the dog's back where the hair grows in the opposite direction from the rest of the coat. This powerful guard and hunting dog comes to us from South Africa, where its job was to protect its master from unwanted visitors, including armed men and large, roaming wildcats. The Ridgeback is not easily intimidated, but it behaves like a perfect gentleman around its family, although some particular individuals can be exclusive one-man dogs.

The Ridgeback is usually very obstinate and has a strong will of its own. Though it accepts its master as leader and is attached to him or her with profound love, it will try again and again to gain the upper hand. Consistent, intensive, and prolonged obedience training, starting when the dog is a puppy, is therefore essential. The reward will be a watchdog and family dog of outstanding quality. This breed is so strong, smart, and active that reliable obedience is an absolute must. A badly trained Ridgeback simply cannot be tolerated. Trying to keep the Rhodesian Ridgeback as an indoor dog is usually a bad idea because this deprives the dog of the opportunity to develop and exercise the skills it was bred for. The Rhodesian Ridgeback is meant for a rural environment, where it can protect its master's land and property.

Common Health Problems

hip dysplasia, osteochondrosis, dermoidism

For experienced dog owners

ROTTWEILER

Height	male: 24–27 in (61–68 cm); female: 22–25 in (56–63 cm)
Weight	male: approximately 110 lbs (50 kg); female: approximately 92 lbs (42 kg)
Coat	coarse, short, flat to the body
Color	black, with rust markings on cheeks, muzzle, chest, legs, above the eyes, and under the tail

Grooming

1	2	3	4	5	6	7	8	9	10

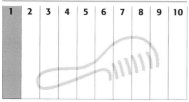

Required Exercise

1	2	3	4	5	6	7	8	9	10

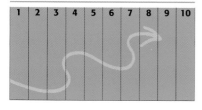

Suitability for City Living

1	2	3	4	5	6	7	8	9	10

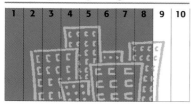

Common Health Problems

hip dysplasia, cancer, heart disease, rupture of cranial cruciate ligament

For experienced dog owners

The **ROTTWEILER** is a German dog and consequently a serious creature; ideally it is quiet, even-tempered, obedient, easy to teach, and brave. Physically a very strong dog with a pronounced sense of right and wrong, it will, if it thinks it necessary, leap to its master's and family's defense without a moment's hesitation. For this reason, Rottweilers must be well socialized from the time they are puppies. Some people claim that there is nothing this breed can't learn. The Rottweiler is not a fast learner, but once it has mastered something, it will never forget it. It is a highly intelligent dog, affable, and not hysterical. Rottweilers are tough and hardy dogs that thrive out of doors and are not as well suited for indoor life. They think of themselves as working dogs, having been bred to drive cattle or function as police, watchdog, and guard dogs. If kept merely for reasons of prestige, and if not given enough exercise and work to do, Rottweilers become tense and moody and are, consequently, not altogether safe to have around. Breeders who raise Rottweilers as guard dogs should be avoided because they tend to neglect to develop the qualities necessary in a family dog, and dogs from such kennels can be truly dangerous.

Height	male: at least 28 in (70 cm); female: at least 26 in (65 cm)
Weight	120–200 lbs (55–90 kg)
Coat	long-haired variety: medium-long, smooth or slightly wavy; short-haired variety: very dense, guard hair lying close to body, thighs slightly bushy
Color	white with red patches, dark markings on head

Grooming

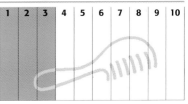

1	2	3	4	5	6	7	8	9	10

Required Exercise

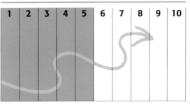

1	2	3	4	5	6	7	8	9	10

Suitability for City Living

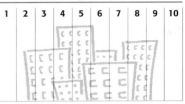

1	2	3	4	5	6	7	8	9	10

The **SAINT BERNARD** is probably the world's most famous canine, depicted as it is in children's books with a small keg of whiskey tied to the neck or locating and rescuing people buried under avalanches. The monks of the hospice on the Saint Bernard Pass in the Swiss Alps bred the Saint Bernard specifically for finding travelers who had lost their way. The first report we have of these dogs rescuing people from an avalanche is from the year 1786. The dogs were originally short-haired because snow sticks to long fur in clumps. In the nineteenth century, the Saint Bernard was brought to England, where it became all the rage. Commercially minded breeders exploited its popularity, upping the price and breeding ever larger and heavier dogs, to the point where some of the animals could hardly manage a normal walk anymore. Using them for rescue work would be inconceivable. Saint Bernards are basically obedient, good-natured, and very loyal dogs, as well as intelligent and courageous. Some individuals have an outgoing personality, but others are very introverted. The Saint Bernard needs close contact with people and daily exercise. Simply placing it in a kennel or run will not do. This dog is eager to please its master and consequently responds well to training, as long as it is treated with respect and patience. Be sure to buy a Saint Bernard from a reputable breeder; otherwise, you may end up with a domineering and aggressive or timid dog, which, given the huge size of the breed, could have disastrous consequences.

Common Health Problems

hip dysplasia, heart disease, entropion, tumors, allergies

For experienced dog owners

SALUKI

Height	23–28 in (58.5–71 cm)
Weight	29–66 lbs (13–30 kg)
Coat	smooth and silky; in long-haired dogs, some feathering on legs and underside of tail
Color	white, cream, fawn, golden, red, gray and tan, tricolor, black and tan, multicolored

Grooming

Required Exercise

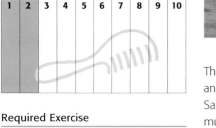

Suitability for City Living

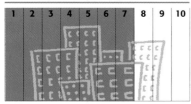

Common Health Problems

For experienced dog owners

The **SALUKI**, one of the oldest domesticated dogs, is named after an ancient Arabian city that no longer exists. The Muslims considered the Saluki a gift from Allah and regarded it as the only holy dog. A number of mummified Salukis have been found in Egyptian tombs. The Saluki moves with incredible speed and was, in earlier times, used to run down gazelles. Tireless and very rugged, it is not deterred by the worst weather or the roughest terrain. At home, it is quiet and aristocratic and, though very loyal to its master, not particularly demonstrative in expressing either love or dislike. The Saluki is more self-preoccupied than any other breed and does not really need people. It is friendly toward those it knows, but trying to keep it together with small children is probably not a good idea. The Saluki is a very strong-willed animal that has had its own way for thousands of years. Any prospective owner of a Saluki has to be aware that the training of this obstinate, sensitive, and easily spooked dog is difficult, and will require lots of time, patience, and above all else, praise. But subordination lessons are a wonderful way of strengthening this dog's self-confidence. Whether a Saluki can ever get enough exercise in a city is an open question. This dog has to be able to walk or run many miles daily. Exotic, stubborn, and elegant, the Saluki is a very special dog for a person with special qualities.

Height	male: 20–22 in (50–55 cm); female: 19–21 in (48–53 cm)
Weight	44–66 lbs (20–30 kg)
Coat	soft, medium-long; with dense, wooly undercoat and harsher, weatherproof guard hair
Color	white, cream

With its big, brown eyes and smiling expression the **SAMOYED** is practically irresistible. But don't be deceived by looks. This dog is not a placid, cuddly teddy bear. It is, first and foremost, a working dog. Explorers like Scott and Amundsen relied on its survival instinct when they set out on their Polar expeditions. At the same time, Samoyeds have none of the aggressiveness found in other sled dogs, but are so gentle that they make excellent therapy dogs. Samoyeds love people, especially children, and need to live in very close contact with their family. They are dignified, obedient, and affectionate. They have a reputation for stubbornness and obstinacy, but this arises from a misunderstanding: In order to perform an exercise they first have to understand what is being asked of them. Yanking a Samoyed around on a choke collar will only result in the dog trying to defend itself, and getting hysterical. If, instead, you use rewards, the Samoyed will follow you to the North Pole, and will, without a moment's hesitation, throw itself between you and any grizzly that might attack you. Samoyeds place high demands on their owners in every respect. They want to be given new tasks all the time and need a great deal of physical activity, as well as time-consuming grooming. Only someone who has been around a Samoyed at a time when its new fur was growing in has any idea how much hair this dog sheds in the process. The hair, by the way, is white with a nice sheen and can be spun into wool and made into sweaters.

Grooming

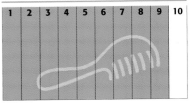

Required Exercise

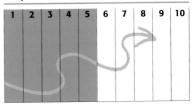

Suitability for City Living

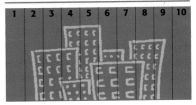

Common Health Problems

hip dysplasia

Suitable for first-time owners

SCHNAUZER

Height	standard: 18–20 in (45–50 cm); miniature: 12–14 in (30–35 cm)
Weight	standard: 33 lbs (15 kg); miniature: 11–18 lbs (5–8 kg)
Coat	hard, rough, with thick undercoat
Color	salt and pepper (in all shades of gray), black

Grooming

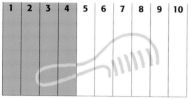

1	2	3	4	5	6	7	8	9	10

Required Exercise

1	2	3	4	5	6	7	8	9	10

Suitability for City Living

1	2	3	4	5	6	7	8	9	10

Common Health Problems

hip dysplasia in the Standard Schnauzer

Suitable for first-time owners

The **SCHNAUZER** is really a rough-haired Pinscher and owes its name to its magnificent beard. The Standard Schnauzer used to be a very popular breed in Swabia in southwestern Germany, where it lived under modest circumstances. It was kept on farms as a watchdog and to catch rats. In keeping with this background, even the Miniature Schnauzer has preserved the breed's unpretentious nature. The Schnauzer is honest, brave, affectionate, daring, and faithful. It is a very lively dog without being restless or nervous, but does need things to do and long walks, no matter what the weather. It loves both work and play, and immerses itself in any situation completely and with boundless enthusiasm. The Schnauzer is definitely intelligent, but also wily, willful, and stubborn, with a rare sense of humor. It needs consistent subordination training with periodic refresher lessons. The teaching has to be firm and authoritative, but done kindly because the Schnauzer will respond with instant rebellion if it is yanked by the collar. Its all-consuming desire is to be included in its people's doings, and it therefore will adjust to any living conditions. It will make the best of wherever it finds itself as long as its people take it as seriously as it takes itself. The Schnauzer is an excellent watchdog and can learn anything required to be a pleasant member of the family.

Height	28–32 in (71–81 cm)
Weight	male: 84–106 lbs (38–48 kg); female: 66–79 lbs (30–36 kg)
Coat	hard, hair 4 in long
Color	dark gray to sandy-red, red fawn, brindle

The **SCOTTISH DEERHOUND** is a giant among dogs. In the legends of the Scottish Highlands, it is always depicted as the noblest of all dogs, a combination of sensitivity, boundless courage, gentleness, and aggressiveness. It is a wonderful companion. It seems to have a good sense of its own size and is, therefore, a good playmate for children, though a small child should not be left unattended near a rambunctious Deerhound puppy. The Deerhound is affectionate, even-tempered, quiet, and polite. It never bites and never behaves unpredictably or with meanness. It approaches strangers with some suspicion, checking very carefully whether the arriving visitors are in fact welcome. The Deerhound takes friendship and belonging together very seriously. Owners should never forget that the Deerhound was kept in earlier days for hunting and that it doesn't take much for these old instincts to be reawakened. Though the Deerhound is gentle with other animals in its own household, a neighbor's cat, once espied, is not likely to escape unscathed. Because this dog wants more than anything else to be close to its people, keeping it in the city is not completely out of the question, if it gets enough exercise and if you have a house or apartment with a floor area of several hundred square feet. However, living in the country or accompanying horseback riders on a regular basis is much more in keeping with the Deerhound's nature.

Grooming

1	2	3	4	5	6	7	8	9	10

Required Exercise

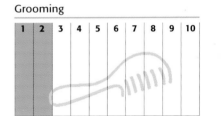

1	2	3	4	5	6	7	8	9	10

Suitability for City Living

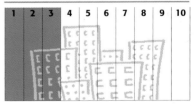

1	2	3	4	5	6	7	8	9	10

Common Health Problems

twisted stomach, torn ligaments

For experienced dog owners

SCOTTISH TERRIER

Height	10–11 in (25–28 cm)
Weight	21 lbs (9.5 kg)
Coat	hard, dense, rough, with soft undercoat
Color	black, brindle, wheaten

Grooming

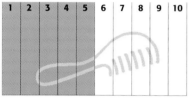

1	2	3	4	5	6	7	8	9	10

Required Exercise

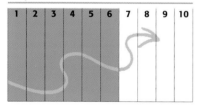

1	2	3	4	5	6	7	8	9	10

Suitability for City Living

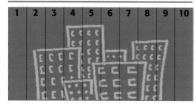

1	2	3	4	5	6	7	8	9	10

Common Health Problems

Scottie cramps, epilepsy

Suitable for first-time owners

The **SCOTTISH TERRIER** was the fashionable dog of the 1930s, when it was commonly featured on whiskey bottles and greeting cards. After that it almost disappeared. The Scottie is a dog for individualists. It is a showoff that always has a thousand urgent things to do, a big dog on short legs, a tough rat catcher, absolutely fearless, and hard to impress. It loves and defends its family, but looks upon newcomers with skepticism, and upon strangers with downright arrogance, simply ignoring them. If it grows up with children, it becomes a magnificent playmate for them that will join in any game, putting up with stoic patience while being dressed up for hours at a time and pushed around in a baby carriage. It has an absorbing life of its own, and you therefore can't expect absolute obedience from it. It will come when called, but instead of taking the most direct route, it lets itself be sidetracked by all kinds of things it hadn't noticed before, such as pebbles, bottle tops, and whatnot. The Scottish Terrier is not easy to train. When given a command, it first considers whether obeying *right now* is worth its while. Teaching has to be started early and done consistently, but in a kind and gentle manner. The Scottie can't be drilled to perform and becomes introverted if trained too sternly.

Height	approximately 10 in (26 cm)
Weight	22–24 lbs (10–11 kg)
Coat	hard, long guard hair with soft undercoat
Color	pure white; markings on the head permitted

The **SEALYHAM TERRIER** is a dog for an individualist. It is a joker with a huge personality, willful, independent, strong, and very purposeful. It is one of the few terriers that does not bark indoors, even though it is a good watchdog and always detects anyone approaching the house. It loves its family, but is very reserved toward strangers. Because the Sealyham hardly sheds at all, it is a great indoor and city dog. But its coat has to be trimmed regularly—never shorn because that makes the hair too soft. The Sealyham Terrier is a very robust, tough, and combative little dog that needs long walks. But don't let it run loose in the countryside, particularly in rabbit country, because it still has the terrier hunting instinct. Training the Sealyham requires patience because this dog is headstrong and stubborn. It quickly figures out the weaknesses of the person issuing commands, but will recognize its master's authority once it has had concrete proof of his or her leadership qualities. The Sealyham displays a great sense of humor even in the act of disobeying, but this is no reason not to train it firmly and consistently, starting early.

Grooming

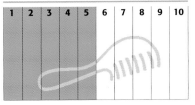

1	2	3	4	5	6	7	8	9	10

Required Exercise

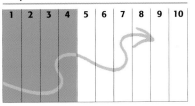

1	2	3	4	5	6	7	8	9	10

Suitability for City Living

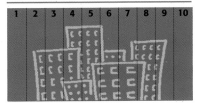

1	2	3	4	5	6	7	8	9	10

Common Health Problems

skin problems, deafness

Suitable for first-time owners

SHAR-PEI

Height	18–20 in (45–50 cm)
Weight	44–55 lbs (20–25 kg)
Coat	short and hard
Color	fawn, sable, cream, black, red, silver, chocolate

Grooming

1	2	3	4	5	6	7	8	9	10

Required Exercise

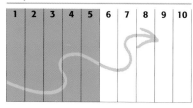

1	2	3	4	5	6	7	8	9	10

Suitability for City Living

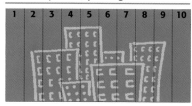

1	2	3	4	5	6	7	8	9	10

Common Health Problems

skin problems, eyelid abnormalities, hip dysplasia

For experienced dog owners

The **SHAR-PEI** is an ancient Chinese fighting dog that was a particularly difficult opponent because, if the other dog sank its teeth in its loose skin, the Shar-pei could practically rotate around itself and ward off the attacker. The origins of the breed are unknown, but its blue-black tongue suggests that it has the same ancestors as the Chow Chow. The Shar-pei has a strong personality and a pleasant, quiet, and dignified manner. It is serious, independent, and very clean. By nature vigilant and reserved toward strangers, it has to be well socialized from the time it is a puppy. It needs an experienced trainer with a firm hand who instantly counteracts any suggestion of aggression, and establishes beyond doubt who is the boss. If this moment is missed, the adult dog may turn out extremely headstrong and dominant. In China, the Shar-pei also worked as a hunting and herding dog, and it consequently has to be watched in a rural environment because many Shar-peis chase wild, as well as domestic, animals. Because the Shar-pei tends to be aggressive toward other animals in general, it is best to keep it as an only pet. The Shar-pei is still advertised as a rare breed even though it has been discovered by clever, unscrupulous breeders who "produce" these dogs without regard for their genetic health and mental well-being, and sell them for big money.

Height	13–16 in (33–40 cm)
Weight	13–15 lbs (6–7 kg)
Coat	long, hard guard hair, with a soft undercoat
Color	sable, tricolor (black, tan, and white), blue merle, black; all with various white markings

Grooming

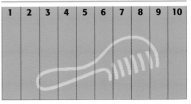

Required Exercise

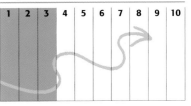

Suitability for City Living

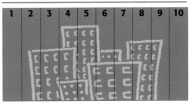

The **SHELTIE** (or **SHETLAND SHEEPDOG**) is probably descended from the Collie. In any case, it looks exactly like a miniature edition of its Scottish cousin. The Sheltie was originally a herding dog on the Shetland Islands, but today it is kept primarily as a lovely and very charming companion dog. It is smart, gentle, obedient, and highly sensitive, which is why some dogs can also be very nervous. The Sheltie is a spirited and active dog, but can quite easily be kept in the city if taken on enough walks or bicycle trips. Reserved and sometimes even timid with strangers, it should be introduced to many different people, and be accustomed to loud noise and new situations from the time it is a puppy. Shelties get along well with other animals, learn easily, and always try to please their master. They react very well to basic and positive obedience training. The Sheltie is a loving and responsive little dog and should never be treated roughly. It responds much better to a cooperative approach and positive reinforcement than to punitive measures. Anyone wishing to acquire a Sheltie should do some careful research when looking for a breeder because timid, easily spooked, yippy, and hyperactive dogs are not uncommon among this basically wonderful breed.

Common Health Problems

"Collie eye" disease, epilepsy, deafness in blue merles, heart disease

Suitable for first-time owners

SHIBA INU

Height	male: 16 in (39.5 cm); female: 14 in (36.5 cm)
Weight	22–29 lbs (10–13 kg)
Coat	double-coated, with thick, soft undercoat and hard, straight guard hair
Color	red, sesame, black and tan, and aka goma (red with black-tipped hairs)

Grooming

1	2	3	4	5	6	7	8	9	10

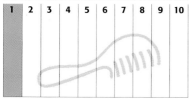

Required Exercise

1	2	3	4	5	6	7	8	9	10

Suitability for City Living

1	2	3	4	5	6	7	8	9	10

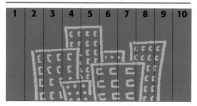

Common Health Problems

hip dysplasia

For experienced dog owners

The **SHIBA INU** is one of the oldest dog breeds of Japan with a history that goes back to the fourth century B.C. Its name means "little bush dog" and derives from its use as a small hunting dog. The Shiba Inu is not for people who want a retiring, unobtrusive dog. It is not afraid of anything or anyone, utterly charming with people it knows and loves, but sometimes rather aggressive toward other dogs. It is highly territorial and thus an excellent watchdog that announces anything out of the ordinary with great fanfare.

The Shiba Inu is excitable, and anyone who witnesses it in an agitated state for the first time will be astounded, for this dog knows how to yodel. It yodels to draw attention to itself and squeals if it doesn't like something. One might say that it tends to overreact. The noise it produces can make your blood run cold, and thus the first objective is achieved: to delay your reaction. The Shiba has another trick it resorts to when it doesn't want to obey a command: It simply becomes immobile like a statue, stands rooted to the spot, tail pointing straight down. Once it has decided to trust a human being, however, it becomes a bundle of love, full of curiosity, responsive to your moods, and more than willing to adjust to your ways. The Shiba Inu is a rare and unique dog, and just owning it is an adventure in itself.

Height	approximately 11 in (27 cm)
Weight	approximately 20 lbs (9 kg)
Coat	long, dense, with short, thick undercoat
Color	all colors permitted

The **SHIH-TZU** is considered a Tibetan breed but is actually Chinese. It is probably the result of a liaison between a Pekinese and a Lhasa Apso that took place at the Chinese court. In any case, it was the favorite dog in the Forbidden City from the seventh century on. Anyone who has gotten to know a good example of the breed will easily understand its favored position there. The Shih-Tzu is a perfect companion dog for city dwellers with a yen for a pet to coddle. This little dog is all charm and personality: loving, self-confident, and very playful. It prefers the comforts of an apartment to the exertion of long walks, even though it is very robust. Its heart is where its people are and where it can count on being safe, petted, and spoiled. This dog suffers from the heat, and its coat requires regular care. The Shih-Tzu was bred for one reason and one reason only: to be loved, and loving is its greatest talent.

Grooming

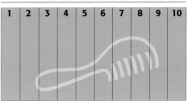

1	2	3	4	5	6	7	8	9	10

Required Exercise

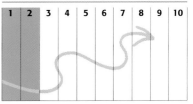

1	2	3	4	5	6	7	8	9	10

Suitability for City Living

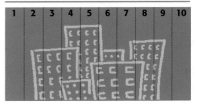

1	2	3	4	5	6	7	8	9	10

Common Health Problems

respiratory problems, kidney disease, entropion, ectropion, ear infections

Suitable for first-time owners

SIBERIAN HUSKY

Height	male: 21–24 in (53–60 cm); female: 20–22 in (51–56 cm)
Weight	male: 45–59 lbs (20.5–27 kg); female: 35–50 lbs (16–22.5 kg)
Coat	thick, double-coated, wooly
Color	all colors and markings permitted

Grooming

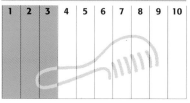

| 1 | 2 | 3 | 4 | 5 | 6 | 7 | 8 | 9 | 10 |

Required Exercise

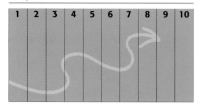

| 1 | 2 | 3 | 4 | 5 | 6 | 7 | 8 | 9 | 10 |

Suitability for City Living

| 1 | 2 | 3 | 4 | 5 | 6 | 7 | 8 | 9 | 10 |

Common Health Problems

hip dysplasia, hypothyroidism, allergies

For experienced dog owners

The **SIBERIAN HUSKY** is a strikingly handsome dog, which is probably the reason why some people who are really not qualified to handle it nevertheless have this dog. The Husky is a true sled dog, and consequently a working animal that needs work to do and, above all, a lot of physical activity. But because it is so very oriented toward humans, the Husky makes an excellent companion dog. It is attentive, very playful, friendly, and normally very good with children. But the Husky is not an easy dog to keep. It is very active and gets bored quickly. It belongs outside in a yard or run that is escape-proof. Having too little exercise and not enough to do makes this dog nervous and destructive. Training Huskies takes a lot of time and has to be done very firmly and consistently since these dogs were originally nomadic, and this past seems to be preserved in their genes. Many Huskies have a pronounced hunting instinct, which can have fatal consequences for the neighbor's cats or chickens. A Husky will test who is boss from the day it enters the household, and if the owner gives the slightest sign of uncertainty or ambivalence, the Husky will immediately move into the alpha position. The Husky needs a master who will work with it (preferably including some roadwork), teach it manners, and prevent it from encroaching on the owner's authority. This dog can either be an utter delight or a destructive terror. The result is up to the owner.

Height	10 in (25 cm)
Weight	10–11 lbs (4.5–5 kg)
Coat	long, silky, glossy
Color	blue or silver-gray with tan markings

Grooming

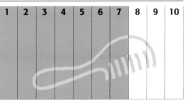

Required Exercise

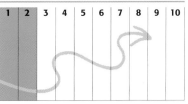

Suitability for City Living

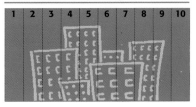

Common Health Problems

Suitable for first-time owners

The **(AUSTRALIAN) SILKY TERRIER** probably came into being through the crossing of Yorkshire and Australian Terriers, but no one knows for sure. In spite of its diminutive size, the Silky is a terrier through and through. It is an active dog that needs a lot of physical exercise. It also tends to be quite demanding of attention and entertainment. But most people who have gotten to know this dog think the effort is well worth it. The Silky is considered primarily a companion dog, but it is also an excellent catcher of rats and snakes. It is very intelligent and extremely fast—both physically and mentally—and, though obstinate, responds positively to obedience training. When you add all these qualities together, you end up with a kind of perpetual mobile. The Silky Terrier is definitely not a low-key dog. It is meant for city people who are active and want a small dog, but one with plenty of spirit and energy. No one has told the Silky how little it is, and it is in fact a giant dog in a small body. To keep its coat looking glossy and neat, the Silky needs regular grooming. When looking for a Silky, you should try to find a breeder who has been raising this breed for several years because sometimes Yorkshires are sold as Silkies, and vice versa.

SKYE TERRIER

Height	10 in (25–26 cm) (but twice as long as it is high)
Weight	25 lbs (11.5 kg)
Coat	long, heavy, straight, with soft undercoat
Color	black to gray or silver, cream; with black on points of ears, muzzle, and tip of tail

Grooming

1	2	3	4	5	6	7	8	9	10

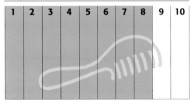

Required Exercise

1	2	3	4	5	6	7	8	9	10

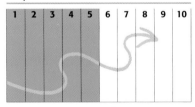

Suitability for City Living

1	2	3	4	5	6	7	8	9	10

The **SKYE TERRIER** is first mentioned in English dog books around 1570, and no less a person than Queen Victoria took it upon herself to breed this dog. For two hundred years it reigned supreme in the London salons, and then it suddenly vanished from the scene, probably because shorter-haired terriers that are easier to take care of caught on. Presumably, the Skye Terrier was created for hunting small predators. It is bold and tough, with a lot of fire and determination. At the same time it is one of the few terriers that is quiet indoors. Its coat requires a lot of grooming and can't simply be ignored. The Skye Terrier is of a steady nature, doesn't like excitement and hectic activity, and wants a lot of attention from its people. Unhappy if it is ignored, it would like always to be included in whatever you are doing and doesn't thrive unless it feels needed. It is not aggressive, but will hold its own if attacked. What matters to this dog more than anything else is its people, to whom it will adapt itself completely. It is satisfied with whatever walks it gets, has practically no hunting instinct left, and is not a barker. Thus, it is a pleasant apartment dog. The Skye Terrier has become quite rare. There are only a few litters per year, something that can only benefit the breed.

Common Health Problems

Suitable for first-time owners

Height	more than 16 in (40 cm)
Weight	35 lbs (15.8 kg)
Coat	silky soft, without undercoat; wavy or curly
Color	wheat-colored

The **SOFT-COATED WHEATEN TERRIER** was Ireland's dog-of-all-work, responsible for herding animals, guarding the homestead, and hunting wild animals. Like many terriers, it is very lively, clever, and playful. Although it is a truly outstanding working dog, it is also a wonderful companion dog and playmate for children. It is an ideal size and adjusts equally well to country and city life, as long as it can be close to its family. It is reliable and more gentle and friendly than most terriers. The Wheaten has to get a lot of exercise or it will become hyperactive. It also needs a lot of attention and a sense of being included. That is why it gets very unhappy if left alone too long. The Soft-coated Wheaten Terrier is generally friendly toward strangers, but may get into fights with other male dogs. It is intelligent, but has one typical terrier trait, and that is stubbornness combined with huge energy. This dog can be difficult to train. If it succeeds in convincing you, while it is a cute little teddy bear of a puppy, that it is a truly delightful lap dog, you will have trouble for the rest of its life keeping it off your bed. So you have to make up your mind early what you are willing to put up with, and stick with your decision.

Grooming

1	2	3	4	5	6	7	8	9	10

Required Exercise

1	2	3	4	5	6	7	8	9	10

Suitability for City Living

1	2	3	4	5	6	7	8	9	10

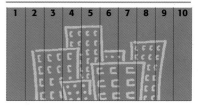

Common Health Problems

hip dysplasia, progressive retinal atrophy, flea allergies

Suitable for first-time owners

STAFFORDSHIRE BULL TERRIER

Height	14–16 in (35.6–40.6 cm)
Weight	24–38 lbs (10.9–17.2 kg)
Coat	short and sleek
Color	red, fawn, white, black, blue, or brindle; with or without white markings

Grooming

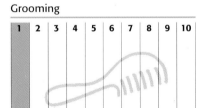

Required Exercise

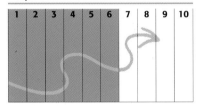

Suitability for City Living

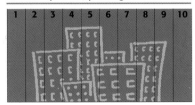

Common Health Problems

tumors

For experienced dog owners

The **STAFFORDSHIRE BULL TERRIER** has a reputation for bloodthirsty cruelty, a reputation that is, however, deserved more by its past owners. In the nineteenth and early twentieth centuries, this dog was bred primarily for illegal use in vicious dogfights. Now that dogfights are fortunately opposed by animal protection organizations and law enforcement authorities, breeders are once again remembering the Staffordshire's good character qualities and are concentrating on obtaining a robust, quiet, cheerful, and very athletic dog. The Staffordshire loves wild play and energetic exercise, but can be kept in the city without adverse consequences. It is fairly stubborn, but it will develop into an obedient companion dog if trained with firmness, consistency, and fairness. This dog must never be struck or encouraged to be aggressive. The Staffordshire Bull Terrier is a small but strong dog with excellent judgment. It needs an owner who can control it, and whose intelligence equals that of this dog.

Height	approximately 10 in (2.
Weight	9–15 lbs (4.1–6.8 kg)
Coat	fairly long, silky double coat, with heavy feathering on legs, tail, and ears
Color	all colors and color combinations permitted

The **TIBETAN SPANIEL** is no more a spaniel than its relative, the Tibetan Terrier, is a terrier. In its country of origin, the Tibetan Spaniel spent its days sitting on the monastery walls and barking at passing strangers. In the winter, the monks carried it around with them under their robes to keep them warm. The Tibetan Spaniel was, from the beginning, a companion dog and a conveyer of happiness, and that is still the job it does best. Not surprisingly, the Tibetan Spaniel is very attached to its people. It is robust, cheerful, lively, playful, and far from a delicate lap dog. It loves to run and horse around, and therefore makes a good playmate for children. It is definitely headstrong, but also sensitive, and responds well to firm but kindly training. It would just as soon not have anything to do with strangers, but is passionately interested in everything that happens within the context of its family. The Tibetan Spaniel is obviously far from passive—how could it be! After all, it thinks the entire world exists just for its own personal amusement. This is a very pretty dog with a coat that is easy to maintain. There is nothing excessive about it: It is small, but not as tiny as a toy breed; its eyes are large like a baby's and its nose short, but not so short as to create breathing problems. The Tibetan Spaniel is spirited and playful, but not enough to get on one's nerves. Relatively rare, the Tibetan Spaniel is an ideal little dog that deserves greater attention, and it will absorb all the attention it can get.

Grooming

1	2	3	4	5	6	7	8	9	10

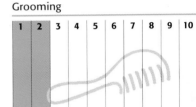

Required Exercise

1	2	3	4	5	6	7	8	9	10

Suitability for City Living

1	2	3	4	5	6	7	8	9	10

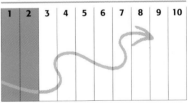

Common Health Problems

Suitable for first-time owners

ETAN TERRIER

Height	14–16 in (35–41 cm)
Weight	18–31 lbs (8–14 kg)
Coat	long, abundant, straight or wavy but never curly; with dense undercoat
Color	gold, white, black, gray; with or without white or tan markings

Grooming

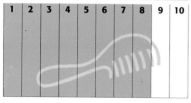

1	2	3	4	5	6	7	8	9	10

Required Exercise

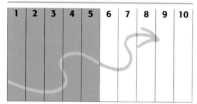

1	2	3	4	5	6	7	8	9	10

Suitability for City Living

1	2	3	4	5	6	7	8	9	10

Common Health Problems

hip dysplasia

Suitable for first-time owners

The **TIBETAN TERRIER** is not a terrier at all, but a herding dog. But that should not stop anyone from appreciating this breed. All manner of legends are associated with this breed, which goes far back in history and is surrounded by an aura of romance. The Tibetan Terrier was the favorite of the Tibetan monks and a highly esteemed gift presented to important visitors. Whatever its past glories, the Tibetan Terrier is a lively, good-natured, playful, and charming little dog. A good watchdog, it often takes its time warming up to unfamiliar people. As long as it is taken on interesting walks, given enough attention, and offered enough fun and games, it will adjust to any environment. But it does not want to be excluded from anything, a quality that contributes to its being a great traveling companion. The Tibetan Terrier can be very stubborn, but generally responds well to fair and consistent training. Its abundant coat requires some care and picks up a lot of outside trash. Particularly on wet days, amazing amounts of sand and dirt are carried into the house, which, once the fur has dried, you will find deposited in little heaps in the places where the dog likes to rest after its excursions. The Tibetan Terrier has to be brushed daily to keep its fur from getting matted.

Height	10–12 in (25–30 cm)
Weight	9 lbs (4 kg)
Coat	short, dense, glossy
Color	black and tan, bright red, chocolate, or rust-colored

The **TOY PINSCHER** is a German dog and, contrary to what many people assume, several centuries older than the anatomically similar Doberman. It is a lively and robust little devil, intelligent, clean, and affectionate.

It is an outstanding watchdog. In fact, it loves to bark and does so if it hears the slightest noise. It is also a terrible show-off, a quality that makes it a great show dog. The Toy Pinscher loves to be the focus of whatever is happening. Even though it is so small, it is well suited temperamentally to be with children—as long as they don't drag it around or drop it. The small bones of these dogs break easily, especially in puppies. The compact little Toy Pinscher is an incredibly strong-willed dog that does best with people who are just as strong-willed and determined as it is. The Toy Pinscher has to be trained very firmly if the owner intends to keep the upper hand over this energetic and pig-headed little dog. Otherwise, the Toy Pinscher will do just as it pleases. However, if you are firm, treat it with respect, and don't deprive it of the illusion that it is a big dog, you will find that you have a terrific dog in spite of its small size.

Grooming

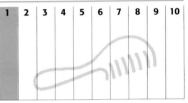

1	2	3	4	5	6	7	8	9	10

Required Exercise

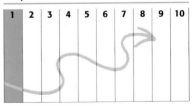

1	2	3	4	5	6	7	8	9	10

Suitability for City Living

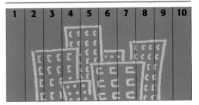

1	2	3	4	5	6	7	8	9	10

Common Health Problems

dislocation of kneecap

Suitable for first-time owners

VIZSLA

Height	21–25 in (53–64 cm)
Weight	44–66 lbs (20–30 kg)
Coat	fine and smooth; wire-haired variety: rough but quite short, lying close to the body
Color	various shades of red

Grooming

1	2	3	4	5	6	7	8	9	10

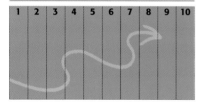

Required Exercise

1	2	3	4	5	6	7	8	9	10

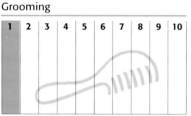

Suitability for City Living

1	2	3	4	5	6	7	8	9	10

Common Health Problems

hip dysplasia

For experienced dog owners

The **VIZSLA** is a special dog meant for special people. This Hungarian hunting dog is an aristocrat, reminiscent of a thoroughbred horse in its powerful yet finely molded and elegant build and its grace of movement. The Vizsla is decidedly willful and determined to test its master's mettle at least once. In this contest of wills, one or the other, either dog or human, will emerge the winner and be the boss henceforward. If you don't want to lose all say about the way the house is run and who gets to sit on the sofa, these issues had better be settled early on. A Vizsla that was not trained very effectively is a pain in the neck for everyone in the household for as long as the dog lives. Also, until it has developed loyalty to its home, this dog is as likely as not to jump out of the window when left alone, simply because life outside looks like more fun. The Vizsla is a poor choice for the city and definitely the wrong dog for physically inactive people. You don't have to be a hunter to have a Vizsla, but you must enjoy very extensive walks and a lot of work and play with your dog. The Vizsla tends to be hyperactive and therefore fits in best with a calm but athletic family, where it can stay in trim shape but feel relaxed. The Vizsla is obstinate and easily distracted, but responds well to firm and low-key training. The name, Vizsla, is Hungarian and means alert and fearless, thus providing further clues to its bearer's personality.

Height	male: 23–28 in (59–70 cm); female: 22–26 in (57–65 cm)
Weight	male: approximately 84 lbs (38 kg); female: approximately 70 lbs (32 kg)
Coat	short, fine, sleek, and dense; there is also a long-haired variety
Color	mouse-gray, silver-gray, or fawn-gray

Grooming

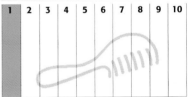

The **WEIMARANER** is an outstanding hunting dog, adept at all aspects of the sport, and if the German Weimaraner Club has its way, this is the way the breed will stay.

The Weimaraner is one of the most elegant dogs, large, self-confident, very intelligent, and with a keen nose. It requires an owner with special talents, and has to be trained well because it is stubborn and headstrong, and will keep testing how much it can get away with. But because the Weimaraner has such irresistible charm, the owner may find it difficult to remain firm, especially in the case of puppies. Any prospective buyer who will be unable to train the dog in obedience and subordination on a regular basis should mentally add the cost of a professional trainer to the purchase price of the puppy. An ill-behaved Weimaraner is unbearable, turning everyone in the house into its slaves. A well-brought-up Weimaraner, on the other hand, enriches the life of the entire family, which it loves and defends. The Weimaraner is a merry and attentive companion with a great sense of humor. It is also a fantastic playmate for children because it loves racing around and chasing balls, and puts up patiently with having Lego pieces stuck in its ears. It needs to be close to its master, and therefore should not be kept in a run or kennel.

The Weimaraner is one of the few hunting breeds that can also be used as a watchdog or guard dog; in fact, some individuals have a tendency to be aggressive. This is a dog that is extremely active, and therefore needs a daily walk of at least two and a half hours.

Required Exercise

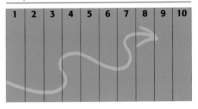

Suitability for City Living

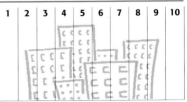

Common Health Problems

allergies, occasionally hip dysplasia

For experienced dog owners

WELSH TERRIER

Height	15 in (39 cm)
Weight	20–21 lbs (9–9.5 kg)
Coat	hard, wiry, and very dense guard hair
Color	black and tan or black and grizzle

Grooming

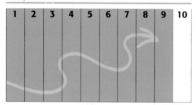

Required Exercise

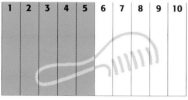

Suitability for City Living

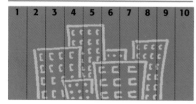

Common Health Problems

Suitable for first-time owners

The **WELSH TERRIER** looks like a miniature Airedale Terrier, but is a separate breed that was obtained in the nineteenth century from a combination of various terriers. It was originally used for hunting animals in their underground burrows, but is today appreciated above all else as a wonderful family dog because it is less pugnacious and violent-tempered than many of its terrier relatives. It does not, however, lack in typical terrier fire. The Welsh Terrier adjusts well to city life as long as it gets enough running, playing, and human company. Its love for activity and people also qualifies it as a dog for children. Reserved toward strangers, it is utterly devoted to its family and makes a good watchdog that does not bark too much. Like all terriers, it is very independent and can, if not prevented, turn into an awful hunter and roamer. Basically, the Welsh Terrier is very obedient and happy to subordinate itself, but because it is also very sensitive, it responds badly to training that is too rigorous. Its tolerance for other animals varies and has to be assessed case by case. It helps if the owner is young and dynamic while the Welsh Terrier is at the same stage of life, for this dog expects its people to fully support and participate in its active way of life.

Height	approximately 11 in (28 cm)
Weight	15–22 lbs (7–10 kg)
Coat	hard, straight, wiry hair, with warm, soft undercoat
Color	pure white

Grooming

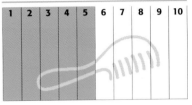

Required Exercise

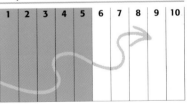

Suitability for City Living

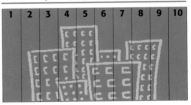

The **WEST HIGHLAND WHITE TERRIER (WESTIE)** is a Scot to its core, but with more than the typical Scotsman's sense of humor. This fabulous little dog has the same ancestors as the Scottie, the Cairn, and the Dandie Dinmont Terriers. A certain Colonel Malcolm of Poltalloch, Scotland, decided around the middle of the nineteenth century to breed all-white dogs after he had accidentally shot a favorite reddish brown dog of his, mistaking it for a rabbit. By now, the Westie has left its hunting past behind, and has become a fashionable companion dog. And no wonder: A real Westie is a cheerful little fellow, courageous in true terrier style, persistent, never shy or timid, ready to join in any foolish enterprise, and not daunted by any new situation. It loves games and toys, rewards, travel, and its master's undivided attention. It has a great deal of personality and is very sure of itself, and therefore has no need to be aggressive, the way many of its fellow terriers tend to be. Its responses are clear and emphatic, but it never snarls or snaps.

Anyone wanting to buy a Westie should carefully check out the breeder. Many dog breeders have, in the past, raised the West Highland White Terrier with the primary motive of making a lot of money, and by now there are a lot of Westies of poor quality around. That is why you should try hard to find a Westie without the flaws resulting from careless breeding. Keep in mind, too, that you will be responsible for the dog for at least 14 or 15 years, so taking plenty of time to choose is well worth your while.

Common Health Problems

flea allergies, dislocation of kneecap, jaw malformations, umbilical hernia, liver disease

Suitable for first-time owners

WHIPPET

Height	male: 18–20 in (46–50 cm)
	female: 17–18 in (43–46 cm)
Weight	20–26 lbs (9–12 kg)
Coat	short and fine
Color	any color or color combination

Grooming

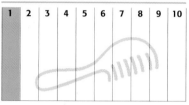

1	2	3	4	5	6	7	8	9	10

Required Exercise

1	2	3	4	5	6	7	8	9	10

Suitability for City Living

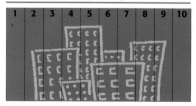

1	2	3	4	5	6	7	8	9	10

The **WHIPPET** is an English greyhound that was, for a long time, called "the poor man's greyhound" (in contrast to the regular Greyhound), and can reach speeds of up to 37 miles per hour in shorter races. In spite of its original use as a hunting dog, the Whippet is a very adaptable family dog, being both a cuddly pet and a hunter. Unlike the Oriental greyhound breeds, the Whippet is easily trained and obeys well. It does not shed and is a perfect size for an apartment. It also loves to play. If there is any monkey business going on, the Whippet is normally at the center of it. It likes children and is easy for children to handle because of its moderate size. The Whippet is happiest if it can live together with another—or several others—of its kind. Then the dogs sleep all tangled up together, something that is hardly ever seen in other adult dogs, except in Pugs. Initially suspicious of strangers, the Whippet quickly lets itself be convinced of their good intentions. The Whippet is of limited use as a watchdog. Although it has an extremely acute sense of hearing and can act as a kind of alarm, it prefers to leave the job of stopping thieves, or other strangers, to someone else.

Common Health Problems

Suitable for first-time owners

Height	approximately 7 in (18 cm)
Weight	approximately 7 lbs (3 kg)
Coat	hair long, shiny, straight, and fine-textured
Color	bright golden-tan on head, chest, and legs; steel blue on body

The **YORKSHIRE TERRIER** was originally developed in Yorkshire to get rid of rats in the narrow passages of the local coal mines. Today's Yorkshire is still a true terrier: proud, lively, merry, yappy, and affectionate. It is a toy breed, but it doesn't know that, and it is better if it is not treated like a delicate flower. It doesn't need long walks, but does want to get outside. As long as its sleeping basket is not kept next to the radiator, it won't need a coat when it goes out. The Yorkshire Terrier is not a Barbie Doll, but a real, rugged little dog that happens to come in a portable size. The time saved not having to take long walks is needed, however, for grooming. The Yorkshire's fine hair has to be brushed and combed regularly. The Yorkshire Terrier has to be trained firmly and thoroughly because it has all the makings of a megalomaniac and tyrant—a trait you, as a human, might possibly find charming, but that other dogs don't look upon kindly. A Yorkshire whose owner picks it up every time another dog approaches will miss out on what is most interesting in life: social contact. Because Yorkies are so popular, it is important to buy from a breeder who keeps all the dogs—not just the puppies—in the house with the family, rather than in boxes in the cellar. Never buy from a breeder whose dogs tremble or are nervous or aggressive.

Grooming

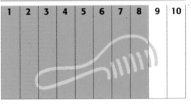

1	2	3	4	5	6	7	8	9	10

Required Exercise

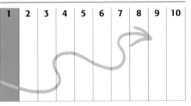

1	2	3	4	5	6	7	8	9	10

Suitability for City Living

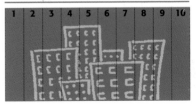

1	2	3	4	5	6	7	8	9	10

Common Health Problems

dislocation of kneecap, eye infections, teeth have to be watched

Suitable for first-time owners

GLOSSARY

Achondroplasia   Arrested development of the long bones

Axonopathy   Genetic disease of the nerve cells' axons, which transmit nerve impulses

Breed   A group of similar individuals whose physical and psychological characteristics are passed on, in pure form, to the next generation

Brindle   Black or darker-colored overlay that produces a tiger-stripe pattern

Cleft palate   An opening or fissure in the roof of the mouth, or in the lips, due to a congenital malformation

Clip   The way a particular breed is groomed by shearing or trimming

Coat   One of the most important external features of a breed; the characteristics are given in the breed's standard

Cocker madness   Nerve disease of unknown cause found especially in red Cocker Spaniels; it results in unpredictable behavior and biting

"Collie eye" disease   A disease of genetic origin that can, but does not necessarily, lead to blindness

Cramps   Painful muscle contractions

Cynology   The science of dogs

Dachshund paralysis   Prolapsed vertebral disc; seriousness of condition varies; there is usually no cure

Demodex   Skin disease caused by the mite *demodex folliculorum*

Dermoidism   Skinlike tissue where it should not occur as, for instance, on the cornea

Dewlap   Loose folds of skin hanging down from the throat and neck

Dislocation of joint   Condition where the ball of a ball-and-socket joint jumps out of its socket

Ectropion   Inherited or acquired abnormality of the eyelid position, with the lid rim turning away from the eyeball

Entropion   Abnormal eyelid position, with the rim turned inward

Fawn   A dark sand color

Hernia   A rupture in the abdominal wall through which an internal organ protrudes (e.g., inguinal hernia and intestinal hernia)

Hip dysplasia   Weakness of the hip joint, leading to changes in the joint; causes painful lameness; the condition is incurable

Instinct   Natural and innate patterns of behavior that are not a response to training or environment

Legg-Perthes disease   Disease of the upper end of the thigh bone; malfunction in the calcification and bone formation process; occurs especially in terriers

Luxation   Dislocation of anatomical structure, as in dislocation of the patella or kneecap

Markings   Areas of lighter or darker color on the legs, the head, and sometimes the chest

Nephropathy   Kidney disease

Osteochondrosis   Degenerative change of bone and cartilage tissue

Pannus   A fleshy membrane that invades the cornea that normally has no blood vessels

Panostitis   Inflammation of an entire bone

Ram's nose   Foreface that appears convex when viewed in profile

Retinal atrophy   Degeneration of the pigment cells of the retina

Spondylitis   Degenerative inflammation of the lining of the vertebrae leading to rigidity of the spine

Standard   A full description of the typical characteristics of a breed as given by the breed's club in an effort to keep the breed pure and to achieve uniformity of physical traits and character. The standard also mentions temperament and uses of the breed

Stop   Technical term for the point between the nose and the forehead, i.e., the step up from the muzzle to the skull bone as seen in profile

Tail   The shape of the tail and the way it is carried depend on the dog's breed

Topknot   A tuft of long hair on top of the head in some breeds (e.g., Dandie Dinmont Terrier)

Toy   The smallest size of a breed that also exists in larger versions (e.g., Toy Poodle)

Trimming   Grooming by pulling out dead and certain healthy long hairs, prescribed in the standard of some wire-haired breeds to enhance the dogs' appearance

Utility dog   *See* Working dog

Withers   The highest point on the upper spine as the dog stands; the distance from the ground to this point is the height of a dog

Wobbler syndrome   Impaired movement such as swaying, staggering, and lack of coordination when walking; occurs in large breeds and is caused by deformation or dislocation of vertebrae

Working dog   Any dog that can perform useful work (e.g., herding, guarding, guiding visually impaired people)

INDEX

INDEX

Photo Credits:

Animal Photography/Thompson: 2/3, 12, 14, 15, 16, 19, 20, 22, 23, 24, 26, 27, 29, 30 (top and middle), 31, 32, 33, 36, 37, 40, 41, 43, 44, 46, 47, 48, 50, 52, 53, 57, 58, 59, 62, 67, 68, 73, 76, 78, 81, 83, 84, 85, 86, 88, 92, 94, 96, 99, 101, 103, 104, 105, 106, 108, 109, 110, 112, 114, 115, 118, 119, 120, 126, 134, 135, 136, 137, 139, 140, 142, 143, 144, 147, 149, 150, 154, 155
Animal Photography/Willbie: 7, 9, 11, 13, 17, 28, 30 (bottom), 35, 38, 45, 61, 65, 66, 72, 79, 80, 91, 98, 117, 132, 138, 145, 146, 148, 152
Bender: 25, 55 (top), 74, 75, 100, 107, 121
Cramm: 113, 128, 153
Juniors Bildarchiv/Wegner: 18
Marek: 87
Reinhard: 6, 21, 69, 77, 82, 93, 123, 124, 127, 131, 133
Rüter: 70
Sander: 97
Skogstad: 1, 4, 8, 42, 90, 116, 122, 141
Steimer: 4, 34, 39, 49, 51, 54, 55 (bottom), 60, 63, 64, 71, 95, 102, 111, 125, 151
Stuewer: 56, 89, 129, 130

Cover and Book Flap Photos:

Front cover: Dannen (2), Darling (2), Reinhard, Steimer.
Front flap: Steimer (3), Thompson (2), Willbie.
Inside front flap: All photos by Animal Photography/Willbie.
Inside front cover: Bender, Reinhard, Steimer, Thompson (2), Willbie.
Page 1: Reinhard, Thompson (4), Willbie.
Back cover: All photos by Animal Photography/Thompson.
Back flap: Willbie, Skogstad, Thompson (3), Willbie.
Inside back flap: Thompson (2), Willbie.
Inside back cover: Skogstad, Thompson, Willbie.
Page 160: Skogstad, Steimer, Thompson (3).

English language edition ©2000 by
Barron's Educational Series, Inc.
Translated from the German by Rita and Robert Kimber
©Copyright 1999 BLV Publishing, Munich, Germany
Original title in German is *Charakter Hunde*.

All inquiries should be addressed to:
Barron's Educational Series, Inc.
250 Wireless Boulevard
Hauppauge, NY 11788
http://www.barronseduc.com

Library of Congress Catalog Card No. 99-69506

ISBN-13: 978-0-7641-1340-6
ISBN-10: 0-7641-1340-2

Printed in China

19 18 17 16 15 14 13 12 11